PRAISE FOR *Secret Keepe*

What a relief as a mom to find a book on modesty that I *know* my daughters will love! Dannah's funny examples and BFF tone will make this an easy read for your tween. It will equip you to have conversations, not confrontations, about hot topics like mini-skirts. Don't let culture dictate what is beautiful to your daughters. Have them read Dannah's book instead.

ARLENE PELLICANE, speaker and author of *31 Days to Becoming a Happy Mom*

Dannah Gresh has always captured the heart and attention of my four daughters and me. Now with *Secret Keeper Girl: The Power of Modesty for Tweens* she does it again by showing girls that true beauty is based on a lifestyle and not their outfits! This resource speaks the language of younger girls, reaches their hearts, and helps them to understand a truth that will impact their future.

WYNTER PITTS, author of *Hello Stars* and *You're God's Girl: A Devotion for Tweens*

Secret Keeper Girl

The Power of modesty for Tweens

BY DANNAH GRESH

MOODY PUBLISHERS

CHICAGO

Unless otherwise indicated, Scripture quotations are from *The Holy Bible, English Standard Version*. Copyright © 2000, 2001 by Crossway Bibles, a division of Good News Publishers. Used by permission. All rights reserved.

Scripture quotations marked NIV are taken from the *New International Version*®.NIV®. Copyright © 1973, 1978, 1984, 2011 by International Bible Society. Used by permission of Zondervan Publishing House. All rights reserved.

Scripture quotations marked NLT are taken from the *Holy Bible, New Living Translation*, copyright ©1996, 2004, 2007, 2013, 2015 by Tyndale House Foundation. Used by permission of Tyndale House Publishers, Inc., Carol Stream, Illinois 60188 All rights reserved.

Scripture quotations marked TLB are taken from *The Living Bible* copyright © 1971. Used by permission of Tyndale House Publishers, Inc., Wheaton, Illinois 60189. All rights reserved.

Emphasis in Scripture has been added.

All websites and phone numbers listed herein are accurate at the time of publication but may change in the future or cease to exist. The listing of website references and resources does not imply publisher endorsement of the site's entire contents. Groups and organizations are listed for informational purposes, and listing does not imply publisher endorsement of their activities.

Edited by Cheryl Molin
Author photo: Steve Smith
Cover and interior design, illustrations of girls by Julia Ryan [www.DesignByJulia.com]

Library of Congress Cataloging-in-Publication Data

Names: Gresh, Dannah, 1967- author.
Title: Secret keeper girl : the power of modesty for tweens / by Dannah Gresh.
Description: Chicago : Moody Publishers, 2017. | Includes bibliographical
   references.
Identifiers: LCCN 2017025832 (print) | LCCN 2017032656 (ebook) | ISBN
   9780802495471 | ISBN 9780802417350
Subjects: LCSH: Preteen girls--Conduct of life--Juvenile literature. |
   Preteen girls--Religious life--Juvenile literature. | Modesty--Religious
   aspects--Christianity--Juvenile literature. | Clothing and
   dress--Religious aspects--Christianity--Juvenile literature. | Body image
   in girls--Religious aspects--Christianity--Juvenile literature.
Classification: LCC BJ1651 (ebook) | LCC BJ1651 .G74 2017 (print) | DDC
   248.8/33--dc23
LC record available at https://lccn.loc.gov/2017025832

We hope you enjoy this book from Moody Publishers. Our goal is to provide high-quality,
thought-provoking books and products that connect truth to your real needs and challenges.
For more information on other books and products written and produced from a
biblical perspective, go to www.moodypublishers.com or write to:

Moody Publishers
820 N. LaSalle Boulevard
Chicago, IL 60610

1 3 5 7 9 10 8 6 4 2

Printed in the United States of America

Contents

Thanks...

irst of all, thanks to all the Secret Keeper Girl moms who are concerned about how this world is making their girls grow up too fast and who want to join me on a mission to keep the little in their girl. This all started with six moms in a classroom at my childhood church. And now we're hundreds of thousands of moms strong across the United States, Canada, and the Dominican Republic, with a smattering of moms from other nations jumping on board.

Next, I'd like to thank two really instrumental dads, my husband, Bob Gresh, and my first publisher, Greg Thornton of Moody Publishers, who initially saw the need for a book on modesty. I am pretty sure it was love for their daughters that made this topic important to them. I wrote *Secret Keeper* for teenagers in 2002, which continues to be a bestseller. We're finally getting around to writing *Secret Keeper Girl* for tween girls, and these two giants among men are still leading with good ideas and encouragement.

Some practical gratitude goes to Jose Pablo and Charo Michelen de Pablo and their daughter, Sharin Pablo de Roca, for giving me their cozy home nestled in the palm trees, where I wrote this book. To be honest, I was stuck until I heard birds singing from those trees, and there the Spirit of God hushed my spirit enough to begin to hear how this book should be formed. I can't thank you enough.

I'm especially grateful for my new friend Judy Dunagan, my editor at Moody Publishers, because she has a great understanding of why this book matters. And Paul Santhouse, whom I have watched pick up the mantle of leadership at Moody with integrity, excellence, and love. It has been a joy to work with editor Cheryl Molin again.

And finally to my delightful team, which always lifts more for me during a writing deadline. Aaron Burrell, our faithful friend and ministry manager, who has brought order and peace to our team; Eileen King, who has been serving Jesus alongside me for more than a decade; Ashley Munn, whose energy, creativity, and contagious laughter always inspire me; Sarah Jones, who along with daughter Jenna vetted this content for me; and, of course, my sweet friend Julia Ryan, who has made every Secret Keeper project "positively" beautiful with her design and illustration. Thank you, friends.

Being A Secret Keeper Girl

❝ *Hey, I wanna tell you something, but you **hafta promise** not to tell anyone."*

You lean in. You can hardly wait to hear what she's going to tell you.

Secrets. The juicy ones, the shocking ones, the embarrassing ones. There's something extra thrilling about hearing a friend's confession. Or getting the courage to tell your own.

❝ *My mom is gonna have **another baby!** But we aren't telling **anyone** until Grandma's birthday because she's gonna be so excited and **we want to surprise her!"**

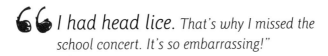 *I had head lice.* That's why I missed the school concert. It's so embarrassing!"

I got Jaycee the **best** *birthday gift ever!* **If you can keep a secret,** *I'll tell you what it is!"*

This book isn't about those kinds of secrets, but another kind. If you look in a dictionary, one of the definitions of the word *secret* is this:

When we use the word **secret** this way, we're saying that we have been taught how to do something or make something, or that we are an expert on a certain topic. Maybe you know

secret *[see-krit] • a method, formula, plan, etc., known only to the initiated or the few.*[1]

the secret to making a loom bracelet *without* a loom or a hook. Or perhaps your mom knows the secret to making your family's famous spaghetti sauce. Or you know the secret to multiplying by nine using your fingers. (That comes in handy for me, since I'm not the best at math!)

In this book, I'm going to introduce you to the seven secrets of true beauty and modesty. And I'm not going to tell them to you so you won't tell anyone else, but so you can keep them alive for the whole girl world.

Why Would You Want to Learn My Secrets?

Because a lot of girls are doing insanely bad things to try to feel more beautiful, and I don't want *YOU* to do those things!

Some girls spend every penny they can get on the latest beauty products.[2] (Don't do THAT!)

Some girls go on diets without telling their moms . . . when they're actually already *underweight*![3]
YIKES! (Don't do THAT!)

Some teenage girls get shots in their lips, making them as big as a watermelon! (Don't do THAT!)

Some girls wear shirts or pants that are too tight, skirts that are too short, and tops that are too low! (Don't do THAT!)

Here's the thing: **it's not working.**
It's been proven over and over again that those things don't make a girl feel better about herself. In fact, I've heard that most women or girls who spend time looking at fashion websites or magazines actually end up feeling more depressed about their own bodies. Who wouldn't? Little of what you see in those magazines is real. The girls are all "lighted," "touched-up," and "computer-generated" to "perfection" . . . a standard that's **IMPOSSIBLE** for you or me . . . or even the model in the picture!

Using the world's standards and ways of beauty to make you feel better about yourself is like trying to quench your thirst with an empty bottle. You're only going to stay thirsty while you become crazy out of your mind wondering why this water bottle is such a bummer!

More importantly, there are things God doesn't want us to do. He wants us to turn away from some choices. In other words, "Don't do that!"

> *"God wants us to turn from godless living and*
> *sinful pleasures and to live good, God-fearing lives*
> *day after day." (Titus 2:12 TLB)*

OK so a little lip gloss doesn't sound like a "sinful pleasure," and a super cute dress is not "godless living." And I want to be really clear: they aren't sinful pleasures! In fact, when my publisher first asked me to write about modesty and true beauty, I said, "No way!" I am a girl who really likes to "shop 'til you drop!" I like fashion, and I was a little afraid of what I might discover in the Bible if I started writing about modesty! Did God want to take away my sense of style?

If you are afraid of this book like I once was, relax! I found out that God didn't want to take away my desire to express my beauty. In fact, the one true God continually expresses **Himself** through beauty. (A sunset over an ocean or the colors of a peacock's tail are two things that come to my mind as beautiful expressions of God's creation.) It's no wonder that we want to do the same thing!

So, grab the cute dress. Sew some funky patches onto your worn-out jeans. Have a facial night with your BFF! These things aren't bad or sinful in and of themselves, but **BE CAREFUL** about *why* you like them. This is where many a girl has gone nearly insane with insecurity about how she looks and obsessions over brand names! **If the reason you need them is to make you feel beautiful,** then you've got a big problem, girlfriend! This is where an interest in fashion and beauty can go wrong and become sinful, as I'll show you later in the book. *The bottom line is that fashion is not where true beauty comes from.* But I know where it does come from. And I know the **seven secrets** that will help you find it so that you will feel confident and aaamazing!

And I'm going to share them with you (and your mom if you're using the *Secret Keeper Girl Mom-Daughter Devos with Coloring Experience*).

AS YOU READ THIS BOOK, I WILL HELP YOU:

 improve YOUR understanding of true beauty & modesty

 increase YOUR awareness of true beauty WITHIN YOU and YOUR contentment with the way that God chose to make you.

 renew YOUR love relationship with Jesus.

You will **KNOW** that you're beautiful just as you are, and you'll know **WHY**.

You will **LEARN** how to recognize lies about yourself and your beauty.

You will **GET CREATIVE** when you dress, fearless of the latest trends & careful in how you present yourself.

You will feel **POWERFUL** when you embrace modesty, because it allows the real you to shine!

♥ (Did I mention that you'll feel *aaamazing*?)

It's time to initiate you into the secrets of true beauty and modesty so you can be an official Secret Keeper Girl! Let's do it.

SECRETS

When You Shouldn't KEEP Them!!!

T he secrets this book is about are the good kind. There are also neutral kinds of secrets: like keeping a surprise party secret or telling your friend that you've always dreamed of being a singer. Those are good secrets.

But there are also bad secrets. Here are three times when you definitely should not keep a secret.

1 When You're Hiding Something and Constantly Fearful Someone Will Find Out

If you worry all the time and even plan your life around a secret, it's time to spill the beans. If you won't accept your BFF's sleepover invites because you still sleep with a nightlight, just get it out there! Say something like, "Okay, but you should know I'm bringing my Sponge Bob Square Pants Nightlight. I never leave home without it." Your friend will laugh and you'll take your nightlight to her house and the secret will die, *but you* **WILL NOT***!*

Or maybe the secret is something you did and you don't want anyone to know. If you're the one who spilled a juice box all over your mom's white carpet, it's time to 'fess up! There may be consequences but it'll be over eventually, and the pain of hiding something will be too.

When Your Friend Tells You a Secret You Don't Know How to Help With

Let's say it's 2:00 in the morning, and everyone at your sleepover party has long passed out. Only your bestie is hanging in with you as you swallow Sour Patch Kids in an effort to stay awake to finish one last movie. Suddenly she whispers, "I want to tell you a secret, but you have to promise not to tell anyone."

She tells you this is the first time in a week she hasn't spent the night all alone because her parents have been leaving her alone at night! Or maybe that she's been using social media and has discovered some really bad stuff. Or that her parents are getting a divorce and she wants your advice on how to stop it.

Should you **keep** her secret?

Sometimes secrets are too big and heavy for you to carry alone. When that happens, you have a responsibility to tell your mom or dad or another safe adult you trust a lot. And if your friend is in danger, you need to do it really fast! They'll be able to help you carry the big secret and help your friend.

3 When Someone Does Something to You and Makes You Promise Not to Tell

"This will be our little secret." Or "no one needs to ever know about this."
If anyone, especially an older person, tells you something like that before they
do something with you or to you—or before they show you something that
makes you uncomfortable—that is a green light to run as fast as you can to the
nearest safe adult. It's a very brave and courageous thing to tell a secret like this.
I'm so proud when I hear one of my Secret Keeper Girls has done this. Stopping
someone like that doesn't just keep you safe, but it can keep other girls—and
boys—safe too! We've got to stick together.

SECRETS will always be around.
There's no end to them,
but you can be wise about
knowing which ones to keep
and which ones not to!

The Master Artist

[You are a masterpiece created by God.]

Worst Day Ever!!!!!!! Today at school everyone was whispering and staring at me. So I went to the bathroom and right there on the tip of my nose was my

...right on the tip of my nose!

first zit. I couldn't get a little cute one, like Laney Douglas' last week. (Hers looked like a beauty mark!) NOOOOOO! Mine is red like Elmo and swollen like a bloated whale. Getting ready for school in the morning used to take five minutes and now it seems like five hours couldn't fix my face! I'm a disaster! It's not like I want to be a lip-gloss addicted beauty queen or anything, but do I have to look like THIS? —Yuzi

Have you ever thought any bad things about yourself when you look in the mirror? Well, **have** you? Let's be honest. You have. And I have too. We're girls, and the whole girl world has experienced the phenomenon known as a bad hair day. And don't even get me started on zits. You know what I think? That God doesn't want us to think those thoughts, and that He really is sad for us when we write them down or worry about them **all day long**.

The Bible tells us that when God looks down upon you, he is *"enthralled by your beauty"*! (Psalm 45:11 NIV). The word **enthralled** means He is captivated, delighted, fascinated, charmed, enchanted BY YOU.

He can't take His eyes off of you. True fact. Psalm 17:8 says you are the **"apple of [His] eye."** That means that if you were to look into God's eye and see the reflection of what He was looking at, it would be **YOU!**

Wow! Think of that. The God of the universe, looking down at your uniquely chiseled features, coloring, and size, keeps His eyes on you because you are one of His treasured creations . . . He thinks you're beautiful.

So why can't you believe it?

Well, somewhere along the way, someone decided to redefine beauty. Right now the standard of beauty is to be as tall as a basketball player and as thin as a pencil. (And don't forget those lips the size of a watermelon.) It's an impossible standard, and as we'll soon discover, the standard of beauty today is a big fat lie!

Here's the deal: no one is both as tall as a basketball player and as thin as a pencil. A tall basketball player's beauty is in her strength. A thin girl's beauty is in her delicate frame, but she isn't necessarily going to be tall! And I'm not sure why people want unnaturally fat lips. (When God makes lips nice and full, they are beautiful! But when we try to fake it, they just look swollen.) If I see you with swollen lips, I'll assume you ate something you were super allergic to. Unless of course God created you with full lips, because then they'll fit your face nicely and you'll be adored for them!

Each of us is different. Every girl has her own special appearance, and there is no mistake in how you turned out. How do I know this? Because I know the first secret—and you're about to know it too!

Secret #1: You are a masterpiece created by God!

Genesis 1:1 reads,
"In the beginning, God created . . ."

Like an artist, He set out to make a beautiful world.

Let's go back to the garden of Eden, where God made the first girl, Eve. Oh wait! Back up. Let's enter the garden just *before* He creates Eve.

Check it out. In Genesis 1, God surveys His fine creation and finds everything just right. He uses the word *good*. The aardvark is good. The aloe plant is good. The alpaca is good. The amoeba is good. The artichoke is good. (And I'm just on the A's, but you get the idea.) *Everything* is good . . . with one exception. He says, "It is *not* good for man to be alone."

Hold it one minute there. Did you catch that? **Alone?** The God of the universe was walking and talking with Adam. How could Adam have been *alone*? God could've easily just been Adam's BFF. He didn't choose to be. Instead, He crafted a masterpiece . . . woman! You are one of those masterpieces. Oh, what a

GOD is a master artist and He created you! THAT MAKES **YOU** A MASTERPIECE!

masterpiece you are! Like the famous Mona Lisa at the Louvre Museum in Paris or a fine Picasso painting on display in Barcelona, Spain, you're a masterpiece worthy of every glance that comes your way!

And there's a lot of glancing going on. Check this out: advertising researchers have actually attached little sensors to readers' eyeballs to follow the visual path and figure out what makes someone spend time reading an ad, increasing an advertiser's chance of sales. Crazy, huh? They've discovered lots of little tricks that will increase the viewing time by 1% . . . 2% . . . maybe 3%. But if you really want to stop the reader, use a woman. I've heard different numbers, but it seems a photo of a woman will increase the length of time someone spends with an ad by up to 30%. That's way more than anything else. It didn't matter much whether it was a woman or a man doing the looking. Both were drawn to the beauty of the female image.

CRAZY, HUH?

Advertisers just don't get the same response when they use the image of a man, no matter how fantastic looking he might be. It's the masterpiece called "woman" that calls our eyes to praise. The masterpiece is applauded by our glances.

You were created as a masterpiece, and **you** are one of God's expressions of beauty. Short, tall; thin, thick; freckles; big eyes, small ones . . . it doesn't matter. The beauty of being an artist is making things that are **DIFFERENT!**

Take a look at these three paintings, and guess which one is by the world-famous painter **VINCENT VAN GOGH**.

The Potato Eaters

Starry Night

Sunflowers

Guess what? They're all by Vincent van Gogh! *The Potato Eaters* is considered van Gogh's first great work of art. (What's not great about something named *The Potato Eaters*!?) *Starry Night* may be his most famous. (Does it look familiar to you?) *Sunflowers* is from his famous still life collection. But each of these is unique in style and use of color. (*The Potato Eaters* is very realistic and dark. *Starry Night* is very unrealistic and used bright colors. *Sunflowers* is kind of in between, realistic but bright.)

Each of them is a masterpiece because they were painted by a master painter.

YOU are a masterpiece created by GOD.

Why are you a masterpiece? Simply because you were created by **THE** Master Artist!

Is it hard for you to believe you are a masterpiece? Do you think you are too tall? Too short? Too heavy? Too thin? Is your hair too curly? Too straight? Too dark? Too light? Yeah, I know how it feels to be different from everyone around you. And how desperate you can become to do something about it!

When I was in sixth grade, everyone in the entire wide world—yep, I'm being dramatic—was getting their hair cut into "feathers." A stylist would cut the hair around your face at an angle so you could brush it back into wispy "feathers" to frame your face. It was *the* style of the day. I had long, straight, blonde hair at the time, and it felt so boring compared to everyone else's. I begged my mom to take me to get it cut. When we did, it didn't go as planned! My hair just didn't want to "feather." Instead it coiled into heavy, greasy-looking curls at the side. I cried myself to sleep a night or two. I felt so ugly.

Determined to fix it, I told my mom that what I now needed was a "perm." Also the rage of the day! My mom said we couldn't afford a salon perm, so I begged and begged and begged until she relented to give me a "home perm." She tightly coiled all my hair into rollers until my eyes teared up and I felt I might not make it through. Then she poured what can only be described as a toxic liquid on my head. I'm pretty sure you could smell me on the other side of the earth. I smelled bad and I looked even worse, but this was going to be what made me beautiful! I could just feel it!

But *feelings are not facts*. Only the Bible can give us the real facts on true beauty. So how about we start there.

Bible **True Beauty** Fact #1

The Bible says one thing that makes a woman beautiful is being different or unique (Song of Solomon 6:9). No matter **WHAT** is different about you, you are a masterpiece created by God. It's not only okay to be taller, shorter, thicker, thinner, curlier, straighter, darker, or lighter, but it is also **BEAUOOO**-tiful! Different is good! (An art gallery full of masterpieces would get so boring so fast if every single one of them were the same, right?)

Bible **True Beauty** Fact #2

The Bible also tells us that a girl in love with Jesus **knows** she's a masterpiece!
"**Wait!**" you might be saying. "**That sounds kind of prideful.**"
So let me put it to you the way the Bible does.

The Bible says a girl who knows Jesus knows **very well** that she is a masterpiece.
That's a lot of knowing. Let me show you where that shows up in the pages of the Bible:

. . . .

Secret #1 Power Verse

"I praise you, for I am fearfully and wonderfully made.
Wonderful are your works; my soul knows it very well.
My frame was not hidden from you, when I was being
made in secret, intricately woven . . ."

(Psalm 139:14–15)

. . . .

This verse says that God, the Master Artist, wove you together when you were still in the womb. Have you ever worked on a weaving loom? Or knitted or crocheted? If you have, you know that you don't just throw a blob of yarn together and say, "Well, would you look at that? Somehow I made a hat!" It takes careful attention to detail to weave something together. It can't happen on accident. It takes counting. Math!

What does that mean for you? Every single thing about you was made *carefully*. God calculated the length of your legs. The width of your nose. The curl in your hair. He's even counted the numbers of hairs on your head (Luke 12:7). He decided what color your eyes should be. And what shade of that color. He chose your skin color and the curves in your bones. You are His piece of art.

God does not make junk. He makes masterpieces. And He wants you to know "very well" that you're a masterpiece.

Why are you a masterpiece? That's simple: to make the Master Artist known. Our primary purpose on this earth is to glorify—or to make known—God. All this creative genius expressed in you is not to make you famous, but to make God famous! (Is this starting to make any sense?)

Let's go back to Vincent van Gogh's work for a minute. He had a unique way of signing his work. He only signed "Vincent." Sometimes it was really big like on this painting at the Van Gogh Museum in Amsterdam.

Seascape-at-Saintes-Maries
by Vincent van Gogh

Van Gogh's Chair by Vincent Van Gogh

Sometimes it was put in an unusual place like on this painting of his chair. See if you can find his name.

See it back there on the drawer? Now look back at Sunflowers by van Gogh and find the unique spot he placed his name on that one! Find it?

All of these paintings tell us "Vincent was here!"

You tell the world "God was here! God is here!"

It is your mission, should you choose to accept it, to let the whole world know that you are a masterpiece created by God **so that the whole world will know God is the Master Artist!**

I really wish I had known this powerful secret before I begged my mom for a perm. Oh yeah, that story didn't turn out so well. My mom had, in fact, rolled the rollers too tightly. So tightly that one of the rollers actually worked with those harsh chemicals to literally shave a spot right on top of my head. At first I could hide it, but as the hair grew, there was a sprout of perfectly straight hair standing proudly on the top of my head. I looked so ridiculous, thanks to my obsession with a hairstyle! If only I had accepted the mission to let the whole world know that God created me very well . . . long, straight hair and all!

Now, let me remind you of something I said earlier. Curling your hair when it's straight or straightening your hair when it is curly is not

HAIR FUN!

bad in and of itself. Have fun! Braid it. Cut it. Curl it. Even color it if your mom thinks that's okay. But make sure that you don't lose sight of the fact that the way God created you is good, and your beauty enables the world to see our Master Artist. It's something He hopes we'll participate in with as much energy (or more) as we use to be creative with our expression of beauty when it comes to our hair!

Secret Keeper Girl

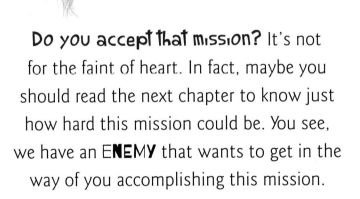

Do you accept that mission? It's not for the faint of heart. In fact, maybe you should read the next chapter to know just how hard this mission could be. You see, we have an **ENEMY** that wants to get in the way of you accomplishing this mission.

The Counterfeiter

[True beauty doesn't come from what's on the outside.]

It was the worst, most-embarrassing moment in the history of all most-embarrassing moments! Laney

... white cotton ball thingies!

Douglas was totally showing off in gym class today. (Probably because Zachary Donaldson, a HIGH SCHOOL FOOTBALL PLAYER, was in the gym working out when we were there!) We were playing volleyball and she jumped up to reach the ball but so did my amazing friend Toni Diaz. When it was over, they were a mangled mess of arms and legs AND ONE LITTLE GLARING CLUMP OF WHITE COTTON BALL THINGIES . . . snagged on Laney's t-shirt!

Toni grabbed it and handed it to her. I've never seen Laney run so fast. I think she ran to the locker room and Mrs. Penland didn't even stop her. People were saying that cotton ball thingy was from her bra! Is it possible that Laney Douglas actually stuffs her bra to look bigger??? :o Sigh! Maybe I'm not that far behind everyone else. (I still want my mom to take me BRA SHOPPING!!!)

—Kate

Here's something I really should tell you: **We are women. We have breasts.** And just like the other parts of us, these will be unique and different from the next person. And yours will grow at a different rate than every other girl you'll ever meet. And they'll end up different, too. This *could* cause no small amount of frustration! You see, most of the bad things we think about ourselves happen when we *compare ourselves to other girls.* (Don't do *that!*)

Thinking bad things about ourselves leads to *doing* insane and silly things.

For example, a very long time ago in Italy, *where God created people to have dark, olive-colored skin*, women wanted to have lighter skin like other women they saw from other countries. They began to use a white powder called arsenic to lighten themselves. SIX HUNDRED WOMEN DIED because arsenic is a poison. Hello! (That's insane!)

That may sound crazy to you and me, but is it really that much different from buying overly padded bras or stuffing your bra with cotton or tissues to look bigger than you are? **(That's silly!)**

tissues for your nose!

If we are masterpieces created by God, we will understand that we do not need to change ourselves with makeup and padded bras. (Okay, it's important to know that sometimes a little padding in your bra is helpful to be modest or to fit properly in an outfit, *but if you're doing it simply to look bigger, something is wrong*.) We don't need clothes, make up, jewelry, fancy hairstyles, and padded bras to make us feel good about ourselves. I said it once, and I'll say it again: there is nothing really wrong with using those things appropriately to express our personal sense of style and to enhance our beauty, but sometimes we become dependent on them *for the purpose of feeling better about ourselves*. We get confused. We think those things are actually what make us beautiful.

To be honest, I think all of us have had moments when we feel like we'll be beautiful if we just have a certain pair of jeans or a specific haircut. If you've had that feeling, you're not alone. **That's why we need secret number TWO.**

Secret #2: True beauty does not come from what's on the outside.

Even though the Bible was written way before blue jeans were the universal statement of style and manicure parties were the rage, God knew they were coming. He knew that as fun as they are, they might tempt us to believe that we *had* to have them to be beautiful. More than two thousand years ago, He had the apostle Peter write this so we would not do silly and insane things.

. . . .

Secret #2 Power Verse

*"Your beauty should not come from outward adornment,
such as elaborate hairstyles and the wearing of gold
jewelry or fine clothes."* (1 Peter 3:3 NIV)

. . . .

OK Let's think: is this verse saying we should all run around naked? No. That'd be completely awkward! Of course God wants us to wear clothing. So if we know that this isn't saying "no clothes," it is also clear that it's *not* saying "no cute hair" and "no jewelry."

The point of this verse is not to make us dress like pioneer women with bonnets and long, poofy dresses! Beauty and fashion aren't bad. If you ask me, God liked expressing Himself with beautiful things. In the book of Revelation, God is described. Things we consider to be beautiful surround Him in John's vision of heaven. Revelation 4:3 says that God sat on His throne, and He was so amazingly beautiful that the writer said He "had the appearance of jasper . . . and around the throne was a rainbow that had the appearance of an emerald." Moses actually saw God's beauty, in part. God's glory was so powerful that Moses had to settle for seeing the back of God. Afterward, Moses's face literally glowed from how powerful God's presence was.

BEA**UTY** is one of God's greatest expressions.

I think it's only fitting that we, created in His image, love expressing our beauty too. So, express it! Use press-on nails. Paint your toes. Find the world's most adorable skirt. Rock a pair of jeans and a graphic T-shirt. Learn to braid. Pop on some lip gloss. Start a bracelet collection. It's okay.

So what IS the point of that power verse? It's to remind us that as fun as fashion and beauty products are, **they are not what make you beautiful!**

[Your beauty does not come from what's on the outside.]

That hardly makes sense to us because we live in a world where we are constantly seeing advertising messages that seem to tell us we cannot be

A PIERCING QUESTION

"Is it okay for me to [fill in the blank]?"

Throughout this book I make a lot of fun references to things like "using press-on nails," "coloring your hair," or "sewing patches onto your jeans." Those are things you should run through your family preference filter. (And by that I mean your mom or dad.) The Bible tells us to honor and obey our parents, so you might have to wait for some things. I wasn't allowed to get my ears pierced until I was 18! But it sure felt good to submit to my dad's preference in that area of my life, and it was super fun the day I finally got to have them pierced!

beautiful unless our hair is cut a certain way or we own a certain brand of jeans or we have the latest trend in jewelry. The message is that what is on the outside is what actually determines our beauty. It's a lie!

Where do those beauty lies come from?

I'm glad you asked!

Do you believe in good and evil? I do. Most of the world does. I mean, show me the civilization that gives out trophies for being a lily-livered coward! That would not make sense to anyone. But almost every civilization recognizes and rewards great lion-hearted courage.[4] That's because humans believe in right and wrong. Good and evil.

We grew up hearing stories that were filled with good guys and bad guys. *Star Wars* and *Cinderella* and *The Lion, the Witch, and the Wardrobe* might not look like they have anything in common.

One is full of star ships and space creatures. One is full of castles and ball gowns. One has talking animals. But they do have something in common: a battle between good and evil. Although these stories are not real, I believe good and evil are very real. Why do I believe that? Because the Bible tells me they are.

Through the Bible, we learn who leads the forces of good and evil.

The Lord God Almighty, our Master Artist, is good (Psalm 119:68).

Satan is a powerful angel who rebelled against God because he wanted to be more powerful than God. He is in a constant battle against God. He is evil (Isaiah 14:12–15).

What did Satan want? To be like God. He is a counterfeiter. That is to say, he seeks to be a fake imitation of the Master Artist.

counterfeit

[koun-ter-fit] • *an imitation intended to be passed off … deceptively as genuine.[5]*

Here's a **strange** BUT **true story**

There's actually a guy who is a pretty good artist named Mark Landis. He's soooooo good, hardly anybody can tell his paintings from the works of famous master artists. (He makes them by painting over copies and pictures of the real things!) Would you believe that he's tricked sixty museums in twenty states when he donated art to them and told them it was actually by a famous artist? In reality, it was painted in his own house by his own hand! He is a counterfeiter. Even though the museum staff carefully examined the paintings, they were fooled. Mark Landis was *that* good when it came to being a counterfeiter! He spent a lot of his life trying to pretend his work was in the name of other master artists.

If God is the Master Artist, Satan is the master counterfeiter. But while Mark Landis isn't an evil man and meant no real harm with the art he created, Satan is very evil and can create a lot of damage in our lives. The Bible says that if we could see him, he would not look evil at all. "Satan disguises himself as an angel of light" (2 Corinthians 11:14).

Satan is not only good at making fakes, but he is good at *faking you out*! He tries to convince you that you are *not* a masterpiece when you really, truly are.

There's one thing you must know about the counterfeiter above all else: he cannot be trusted! The Bible says, "There is no truth in him. When he lies, he speaks out of his own character, for he is a liar and the father of lies" (John 8:44). One of his favorite things to lie to you about is your value! He wants to convince you that you are NOT a masterpiece created by the Master Artist. If he can do that, the world won't see you and remember God. Remember, that's the true purpose of your beauty . . . to remind people, "God was here! God is here!"

Expect to be lied to when it comes to beauty in general. Case in point: almost ANY photo you see on the Internet, billboards, posters, advertisements . . . is one big fat LIE! The tricks of the trade really have to be SEEN to be believed . . . so let me introduce you to the leading photo-altering program, Photoshop. Using it, we can make almost anything look real. Check this out:

Did you know you could ride roosters?

You didn't? Well, of course you can't! That's a picture of me riding a horse combined with a picture of my crazy rooster, Franklin. My designer friend, Julia, put them together, and suddenly I'm riding a rooster!

Cock-a-doodle-WHO?

ALENA is not only the young star in *War Room*, but also (along with her amazing mom Wynter) a new author of some fabulous fiction books under the series name *Lena in the Spotlight*. Check them out!

The lies we see about beauty are very subtle, but no less real. And I'll take this photo of my beautiful and perfect-just-as-she-is friend, Alena Pitts, who was the young star of the *War Room* movie with her auntie Priscilla Shirer.

Let's make her look different using Photoshop. We've thickened her hair, widened her eyes, and changed her cheekbones. This isn't real! (And frankly, I like the REAL Alena better than the fake one!)

The Real ALENA

ALENA Photoshopped

YIKES! This is crazy, right? Sadly, a lot of the photos you see in ads and even on Instagram are equally fake!

More than a few famous advertisers have gotten into a lot of trouble when its designers went too far with Photoshop. Often these models end up looking so skinny they don't even look real. They take way too much away for us to be fooled.

This is **JUST** ridiculous! Don't you agree??? Girls, you don't have to change yourself to be beautiful!!! You are perfectly crafted just the way you are.

{ So, if beauty doesn't come from our hairstyles, jewelry, and fashion, where does it come from? I'm so glad you asked! It's one of the most important things a girl can know, and it's our **THIRD** secret. }

Franklin, the rooster, and me riding Truett before I transformed into the ... Notorious Chicken Rider of the East!

The Confusion

[True beauty is not about how you look. It's about how you see.]

...no idea what happened!

What ON EARTH happened to me??? As far as I can tell the earth opened up and swallowed my fashion-obsessed brain. The next thing I knew my heart grew two sizes, and I was throwing the pageant. You know the pageant I was BORN TO WIN . . . the one I've been waiting for since before I could talk. I have no idea what happened to me backstage. But I just saw things differently, like someone put super mega-powered vision glasses on me and I could see right into Riley Peterson's inner being. Her dress didn't meet the pageant rules! How could she have missed it? I knew one thing: she needed my one-of-a-kind Cinderella-worthy dress way more than I did. So, before I knew it I was wearing her dress—the one that got me disqualified. And she was wearing my show stopper! The Miss Teeny Pop Crown will never be mine. (And don't tell anyone, but I feel pretty good about that!) —Danika

Where DOES real beauty come from if you can't buy it at the mall? We've already learned that it *doesn't* come from the outside, right? So, we've got to go much farther than the mall and deeper than your closet to find something that will make you truly beautiful. For one thing, what people think is beautiful on the outside is always changing.

Fashion trends change from culture to culture and season to season. Sometimes the things one culture finds appealing make another laugh. In Madagascar, a woman's exposed arms were once considered very sexy, so you were a *wild* woman if you wore short sleeves.

In the Bible we read that a nose ring was presented to Rebekah as a sort of engagement ring when she agreed to marry Isaac. It said way more than "marry me." It also said, "I'm rich." A nose ring was reserved for the upper class and was a sign of wealth. You won't find our First Lady wearing a nose ring, because they don't mean the same thing in our culture today.

More recently, some of your grandmas and moms were wearing what we know as "ugly sweaters." (Only they didn't think they were so ugly!)

All I'm saying is that what is in style today might be something you laugh at in just a few years. Girls, we've got to stop getting so obsessed with what we look like on the outside. The world WILL keep spinning if your jeans don't have the most popular name brand on them! You can't measure beauty simply by what is or is not on the body. True beauty comes from deep inside of you.

You remember that power verse from the last chapter? It said: "Your beauty should not come from outward adornment, such as elaborate hairstyles and the wearing of gold jewelry and fine clothes." Get ready for the verse that comes right after it, because it's your next power verse. (You can't fully understand one without the other!)

Secret #3 Power Verse

"Be beautiful inside, in your hearts, with the lasting charm of a gentle and quiet spirit that is so precious to God." (I Peter 3:4 TLB)

When you see these verses together, it's even more apparent that God isn't dissing fashion so much as He is calling you and me to a deeper, truer beauty than we can get at the mall.

The fashion **INSIDE OF US** is what makes us **GORGEOUS** in the eyes of God! Oh, yes, you can wear "clothes" on the inside like kindness . . . helpfulness . . . encouragement . . . love . . . forgiveness . . . and so much more! **THESE** are the things **GOD** thinks are fashionable. And He likes it when we accessorize with some laughter . . . and hugs . . . and high fives for each other!

Unlike fashion and external beauty, our power verse says that inner beauty is "lasting." Some versions of the Bible say it is "unfading." This *could partly* be referring to the fact that we're all gonna get older some day and this changes the way we look, but I think it has very little to do with age. This is something worth exploring, so let's pretend you know two identical twins. Physically, they look like the same person. Not a thing about them is different, down to the itty, bitty beauty mark on their right cheek and the funky zig-zag part their hair naturally falls into. Both of them are dressed well and physically attractive, but there *are* some differences . . . *beneath* their skin.

Twin #1: Fading Beauty

Twin number one is a mean girl. She's this way mostly because she's insecure and jealous and doesn't really like herself nearly as much as she pretends. When she looks in the mirror each day, she obsesses over how she looks, and she HAS to have designer jeans or she'd just die of embarrassment. On a daily basis, she's worried about who likes her, but she wouldn't notice a lonely classmate if she had super vision x-ray glasses. She's much too busy looking out for herself to see the needs of others. The more time you spend around her, the more something happens to the way she appears to you. **Her beauty fades.**

> External beauty is hard to see over **INTERNAL UGLY!**

Have you ever met someone like this whose stunning looks *fade* as her personality comes through? Then you've seen the girl who lacks true beauty. External beauty is hard to see over internal ugly!

Twin #2: Unfading Beauty

Twin number two is sweet, kind, and helpful. She's confident in who she is, so she doesn't spend much time in front of the mirror worrying about how she looks, and she likes the challenge of finding a bargain when it comes to fashion because she knows it helps her mom and dad afford other things. A lot of people like her because she's always making others feel important. She does this by seeing their needs and helping them. The more you spend time around her, the more beautiful she becomes.

Have you ever met a girl who becomes more and more attractive as you get to know her? If you know a person like this, you've seen true beauty. External beauty shines brighter when inner beauty is growing!

{ External beauty shines brighter when **INNER BEAUTY** is growing! }

These girls look 100% the same to our physical eyes, but the one wearing beautiful inner garments has a beauty that lasts and is unfading. And the one who is wearing ugly inner garments has a beauty that fades away. What's the difference? It's not in the way they look. (They're identical twins!) It's in the way that they SEE!

> Secret #3: True beauty is not about how you **look**. It's about how you **see**.

True beauty has very little to do with how we *look*—our skin, our hair, our legs, our eyes, our figure, and more. It's got everything to do with how we *see* the needs of others. God's Word reads, "Let each of you look not only to his own interests, but also to the interests of others" (Philippians 2:4).

God wants you to have His eyes to see the needs of others before your own needs! This is true beauty. He wants you to be less worried about how you look and more concerned with how you see. The only way you'll grow that skill is to spend more time working on your inner beauty than your outer beauty.

HAVE
HIS
EYES TO
SEE!

My daughter Autumn is a true beauty. Not only did God carefully craft her lovely face—her perky nose and full lips are so sweet—and tiny little body, but He planted beautiful things in her heart. When she was thirteen, one of our favorite families broke up. No other way to say it. Mom left and dad was alone with several children. Autumn **SAW** this suddenly single dad's need.

USE THE EYES OF YOUR HEART!

Often she would ask if we were making him food and if we could help them with their home. She has great vision, and that's where true beauty comes from: your eyes! Not really your physical eyes so much as what the Bible calls the "eyes of your heart" (Ephesians 1:18).

In the same way—if God has marriage in your future, I want a guy to be attracted to your beauty by what he "sees" in your heart and mind. If he is attracted to your internal beauty, he'll also find the physical expression God has crafted in you to be beautiful, too! (Even when you get old and it's beginning to fade away . . . but that's all a long time away.)

I'm going to help you with your vision in just a few short chapters, but for now I want to introduce you to some real live girls who have excellent vision. (Read: true beauty!) Turn the page to the next chapter for a fashion show of the **"INNER"** kind.

Protecting the Masterpiece

[God wants nothing we wear to distract people from seeing our true beauty.]

I was totally sprawled on the ground with no hope of saving a scrap of I-meant-to-do-that-ness. I wished I could snap my fingers and disappear!

... wish I could disappear!

For a millisecond I thought maybe no one would notice the girl lying face-down dressed in a tight, itchy, horrible corncob costume. Yep! My mom dressed me like a COB OF CORN for the annual Popcorn Festival. She thought I would make a good greeter and that it was my duty to God and country to volunteer. She says we're all supposed to do good deeds. But what I did was make a mess because that silly costume was impossible to walk in. My only hope is that the costume was too distracting for people to notice WHO was actually in there! —Yuzi

I'd like to show you some masterpieces and tell you just one way that their true beauty shines.

REBECCA has been given what God calls in the book of Exodus "a spirit of skill" with fabrics. She makes beautiful clothes, bags, and other fabric items and shares them generously with other people. Her true beauty shines through her **GIVING!**

REBECCA BARKER

SHARIN ROCCO

ZAANI ANDERSON

SHARIN has a true "gentle and quiet" spirit, which we learned about in our power verses. I've watched her interact with her group of Secret Keeper Girls in the Dominican Republic and have been blessed by her quiet spirit. Her true beauty shines through her **LISTENING!**

ZAANI is the middle Anderson sister. Sometimes middle sisters get lost in the shuffle, but I watch Zaani confidently be the girl God made her to be while she lets her big sister, Sorochi, shine and helps her little sister, Ru, grow. Her true beauty shines through her **KINDNESS!**

JENNA JONES

JENNA loves the Lord, and her parents have been teaching her how to manage her weekly allowance to demonstrate it. When they asked her where she wanted to donate some, she prayed and felt led to give it to my Secret Keeper Girl-to-Girl fund, which helps girls in need. Just a week later, a hurricane hit Haiti, and I was able to send Jenna's gift and the gifts of many others to help some girls whose home was damaged. Her true beauty shines through her **FAITH!**

These girls wear beautiful things *inside*. And that is precisely why they are careful with what they wear on the outside. Let me help you understand by using God's Word. Your next power verse sounds a lot like the verses we have been studying written by Peter. But the verses below are written by the apostle Paul and pack a punch of sheer power at the end.

Secret #4 Power Verse

"I want women to be modest in their appearance.
They should wear decent and appropriate clothing and
not draw attention to themselves by the way they
fix their hair or by wearing gold or pearls or expensive
clothes. For women who claim to be devoted to
God should make themselves attractive by the good
things they do." *(I Timothy 2:9–10 NLT)*

There it is again: the truth that what makes us attractive is inner beauty, which gives us vision to SEE the needs of others and do good things to help them. The purpose of this verse once again is to push us into goodness, not to make a lot of rules about our clothes.

But it *does* mention clothes. And it says they should be *appropriate*. Appropriate means being able to say, "It's okay!" So let's see if some of these things are appropriate.

IS IT OKAY?

Let's start simple: is it okay to wear a party dress to a campfire? Come on, now. People would think you were fairly odd! There's nothing really wrong with it, but if your mom spent a lot of money on that dress and you came home covered in gray ash, she may be frustrated with you. It's just not appropriate to wear a party dress to a campfire. It is appropriate to wear some jeans and a sweatshirt!

modesty

[mod-uh-stee] • *presenting your external beauty so carefully that it does not distract people from seeing the good things you do, but empowers your true beauty to shine*

Now, let's go in another direction with this question.

Is it okay to wear your swimming suit to church? Now, this is starting to feel a little uncomfortable for people around you because you just don't have enough fabric covering you, right? (Of course, this example is so extreme, it sounds more silly than anything.)

Now, let's get to the heart of the Bible verse. Is it okay to wear an itty-bitty skirt that's so unbelievably short that it shows your panties when you bend over to pick

something up? Uhm! No! Now, things are getting way too revealing. It's inappropriate and draws attention to a girl in a way that is not okay.

But each and every day the world is making it normal for you and me to be inappropriate. That is: to wear things that are **NOT OKAY**! Of course, I haven't seen anyone wearing a Speedo to worship, but I've seen plenty of super-short skirts on girls. You know what I mean?

God gives us specific instruction not to wear something that is immodest or inappropriate. Why? Not because He likes making up lots of rules about clothes, but because He wants nothing about the way we dress to distract from the good work that we do for Him. That's why we have to be careful and appropriate in the way that we dress. It's time to talk about the power of modesty!

Modesty is a power that protects the ability of others to see God's good works in your heart and through your life.

It is not meant to hide your body, but to reveal the true beauty that grows within you.

Immodesty carelessly reveals too much of your body and distracts people from seeing what's inside of you! *It takes away the power of your inner beauty.* You see, the power of modesty is that it lets people see inside of you. But there's a lot of immodesty in our world. In fact, it's more normal to see a lot of girls who are immodest than it is to see a lot of girls doing good things for other people.

WARNING:

Some people make modesty all about a lot of rules for our bodies. "Your skirt should be two inches above your knee." My definition of modesty is a bit different because I think it has a whole lot more to do with our hearts and why we choose a skirt, not how long it is. You won't find this definition in a dictionary, but I believe it expresses God's definition of modesty accurately.

A Brief History of Modern Immodesty[6]

Fashion has always been cycling from modest to immodest. Here's a look at how the progression goes.

It All Began with a Dress

1913 · Rounded & V-Shaped Necklines After a season of strict modesty accompanied by ordinary dresses having high collars, clergymen all over the world jumped into their pulpits to condemn the new rounded and high v-necklines women were sporting. (Gasp!)

1918 • Pants

When World War I hit, so did a fashion item that had been trying to catch on since fourth-century Persia: women's pants. Since women needed to go into factories to do men's jobs, this time the fashion statement stuck. Loose pants and riding pants were the rage!

1920 • Flapper Dresses

For the first time, dresses were short . . . and women were showing ARMS & LEGS! "Flappers," what the girls who wore these dresses were called, were known to attend "necking parties" where they randomly kissed any guy they met. The dress, though modest by today's standards, was a symbol of their rebellion.

1960 · The Mini-Skirt

The mini-skirt was the first fashion item marketed directly at the teenager. Fashion designer Mary Quant saw that young women had to "dress like their mothers" and wanted to give them their own fashion sense. The skirt became a symbol of women's freedom and rebellion. (There's that word again.)

1970 · Bare Midriff

The West was finally introduced to the female belly button. Low-riders cantered in to pair up with shirts that showed off the curves of a woman's body, and became a fashion statement that comes and goes—almost as unstoppable as the mini-skirt.

2000 · Underwear as Outerwear

Underwear was no longer under anything. First glimpsing out over the low-cut collars of women, it slowly made its way to the surface. A camisole, bra, or thong "whale tail" was considered a fashion statement rather than an "oops!"

TODAY · Anything Goes

Taking a little from each fashion decade, today a girl can wear just about anything, and it's considered nothing more than an expression.

I need to confess to you that I've had some moments in my life when I gave up the power of modesty. I didn't protect my internal beauty by presenting my body carefully.

Once, I stood up in the front of my minivan, the door wide open, while I bent over the seat to reach my stuff. It was a loooong reach. As I turned to slam the door shut with my arms loaded, I noticed a guy sitting in his car right beside me with his jaw dropped so low that his mouth looked like the Grand Canyon. His face was red when I caught him staring.

That's when the draft hit me. A cool spring breeze announced to me that the hem of my very short skirt was wrapped up around my waist and my panties were the featured view. You can guess who was blushing then!

THAT'S WHEN THE DRAFT HIT ME.

Let me tell you that no one who saw my lacy underwear was going to notice that I was a good person who loved serving her community and doing good things for Jesus. My clothing distracted them from seeing the good things I did. I don't wear skirts that short anymore. Lesson learned! I have embraced the power of modesty. I want people to see the good things I do *because I want them to see Jesus in me.*

Modesty and the way it distracts us from seeing inside a person is actually quite scientific! Let me tell you about the Gestalt theory. (Warning: college-level thinking ahead! I believe you can handle it.) The Gestalt theory teaches an artist to control a viewer's time by forcing the person to mentally complete a visual image. Because the brain is intrigued by completing the incomplete, it will always pause to finish an unfinished picture. **Check out this trio of circles. What else do you see?**

You think you see a triangle, because that's the most common image that your brain wants to use to complete this.

Check out this next little graphic. Describe what you see.
People say they see a person, even though this is just a couple of curved lines and a dot. Why? We naturally seek to continue visual elements.

Now check out this photo of clouds in the sky. What do you see?
You probably have sat in the grass and looked up at clouds to find things and seen anything from a puppy, to a crown, to an alligator, or Jesus riding on a white horse. There's

a name for what's happening in your head. It's the Gestalt principle of continuity. (Now that's college student stuff, right there. We're smart!)

Now, let's apply that to the way we dress. What does someone see when a girl walks by wearing a long, tight skirt with a slit all the way up the sides? They see past the fabric, because the slit invites them to finish the picture. This is simple visual science.

When our imagination kicks in and we start being focused on a person's body, we have a hard time seeing their heart. That's how we get distracted from seeing a person's good deeds! (Does this start to make the POWER of modesty make some sense? You see, modesty is your choosing to control what a person sees: the outside of you or the inside!)

I think you're ready for secret #4.

Secret #4: God wants nothing we wear to distract people from seeing our true beauty.

Now, don't go all "Little House on the Prairie" on me. Don't hide your body. That's not the purpose of God's instruction on modesty. After all, you are a masterpiece created by God, and masterpieces are made to be seen. You remind people of the Master Artist!

But your true beauty and value lies within you. And it is a treasure to be carefully protected. You must take care to present yourself as a valuable masterpiece.

As the protector of a masterpiece created by God, you are a curator! A curator is a person in charge of an art collection.

curator

[kyoo-rey-ter] • the person in charge of a museum, art collection, etc.[7]

MASTERPIECES, you see, must be protected.

Take, for example, the *Mona Lisa*. She's considered the world's most famous painting and was completed by master artist Leonardo da Vinci in 1517. Today she is *curated* by The Louvre (pronounced "looove"), a famous museum in Paris, France. She's hidden behind a sealed bullet-proof glass enclosure that is almost two inches thick. The temperature inside is permanently set at 43 degrees Fahrenheit and 50% humidity. A tiny spotlight brings out the colors in the painting. During World War II, when art was often stolen by Nazi soldiers, the painting was hidden in five different locations. Though she once traveled to other countries for display, the curator says she will never again be lent out for exhibition, for her protection, due to the fact that she wasn't treated properly in other locations.

This is certainly more protection than she was given in 1911 when she was STOLEN. That's right, the captain of the guard came around to the location where she was kept on a few pegs, and she was simply gone. He didn't freak out or anything. (HELLO! FREAK OUT! IT'S THE WORLD'S MOST FAMOUS PAINTING!) He just assumed maybe someone had taken the painting out for cleaning or photographing for marketing purposes. He did NOTHING to look for her, giving the thief a long time to get away. (It took three years to return her to her proper place.)

Here's the point: you have to decide if you will be like today's museum curator who uses his power to carefully protect the Mona Lisa, or if you will be the careless guard who allowed her to be stolen in 1911.

You deserve special protection and care. Modesty is a power that gives you the ability to have yourself properly and safely viewed. (It's not the only way we protect ourselves, and even then we sometimes have to tell someone older and wiser if someone doesn't respect our boundaries for our body.)

Remember what I wrote about not keeping "bad secrets" in the introduction? If someone is disrespectful of your body, you should tell someone!)

Do you know who is in charge of that special care? **YOU!** I bet your mom and dad are doing a good job of it or this book wouldn't be in your hand right now, but ultimately it will be **YOU** who is put in charge of the art that is **YOU!**

BUT I do think that modesty gets a bum rap these days. For example, recently a school told girls not to wear form-fitting yoga pants. I think that's a perfectly reasonable dress code for school, but some people get all worked up about the "rights" a girl has to wear yoga pants to school and they say that people who teach modesty are "shaming" girls from showing their bodies. I look at it differently. I think we have the "right" and "responsibility" to present ourselves appropriately in all situations. Some yoga pants may be appropriate in the gym, but in an academic setting I want to wear clothes that allow my brain to be the main event! Not my body. In order for that to happen, I need to wear clothing appropriate—or created for—learning, not stretching. This is where we need to understand the importance and power of modesty.

{ Let me share a little bit more about this power of modesty and why it's a wise choice. Let's go to an ART SHOW! }

The Art Show

[What we wear becomes sin when it says "look at me" instead of "look at God."]

ZACHARY DONALDSON LOOKED AT ME! And I think I know why. You know that skirt my Aunt Janet made me?

...it had to be the skirt!

The one that goes past my knees and is the longest skirt you've ever seen in your entire life? Mom said I HAD to wear it today! (Aunt Janet and Uncle Andy are arriving from Lancaster for a visit today.) Anyway, back to ZACHARY DONALDSON! In the bathroom Laney Douglas looked at me with disdain and I just COULD NOT wear that skirt like that all day. Danika McAllister to the rescue. She taught me how to roll the waist of my skirt to make it shorter. And make it shorter I did. WAY SHORTER. (The kind of short I would make it if my mom weren't a prude.) And just when I walked out of the bathroom with Danika, there was ZACHARY DONALDSON looking at me. Really, truly looking at me. It had to be the skirt! —Kate (DONALDSON?)

I don't think most girls think that hard about what they wear. Very few of us go to the mall saying, "Let me find something really immodest to wear!" More likely we think, "Chillax! It's just fashion!"

Is it *just* fashion?

I'd like to push you . . . stretch you . . . challenge you. I'll do it all with just one word. Are you ready? Once I discovered this Hebrew word in the Bible, it changed my thinking about how I present myself. Will you stick with me through this? This is the hard part of the book, so brace yourself. Here we go!

I'd like to talk to you about the word *sin*.

What? I thought we were talking about fashion!

Oh, we are. Focus with me now. Remember, I used the word *sin* at the beginning of the book but then softened things up a bit so you knew that fashion isn't sinful.

But sometimes how we use it and approach it can be. Let me show you what I have learned from God's Word.

> How would you define SIN? Take a moment and really think about it.

Let's see how your thinking lines up with the Bible. Of course, it was originally written in the Hebrew and Greek languages. To really understand the word *sin*, we need to go back to the Hebrew Old Testament.

The Hebrew culture revolved around war, so some of the Hebrew words are archery terms. The main Old Testament Hebrew root word for sin is *chatta* (or *hatta*). To pronounce that you kind of spit out a hard "h" sound and add "atta"! Try it.

[ch-atta!]

It most literally translates
"to miss the mark."

Picture an archer's target. What do you most desire to hit? The bull's-eye! That's the "mark." The intended purpose of aiming your arrow is to hit that prized center mark.

Spiritually, the bull's-eye is anything God intends for you and me. For example, if kindness is God's purpose (and it is), then we "miss the mark" when we are mean girls or frenemies. See?

Of course, in our human minds, when we see someone being a bully, we think: "sinner!"

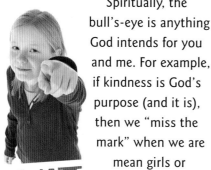

HIT THE BULL'S-EYE!

But God is much more loving than that! He isn't up there saying, "Bad! Bad girl! You really messed up! That was mean." He is up there saying, "Oh, My sweet masterpiece, you missed the mark! That's not how I designed you to act." And because of His love, He offers us forgiveness.

Isn't that amazing? God loves us enough to FORGIVE us, and to let us try again! His standards are demanding. The bull's-eye is small, but His response to sin is packed with far more love than our handed-down definitions.

Let's look at this word, chatta, a little more closely. It's easy to see sin when we see someone miss the target altogether. Murder is a good example.

Can you think of some other sins where the entire target is missed? Add a few to our target above, placing these "big nasties" off of the target.

Did you write things like "lying" or "cheating" or "stealing"? Okay. You're getting it.

Now, you and I both know that sin doesn't have to be this "big" to still be sin. Look at all that space on the target between actually missing the target at all and skillfully hitting the bull's-eye. The meaning of *chatta* doesn't say we "missed the target." It says we "missed the mark"—the dead center of the target . . . the bull's-eye. That's the mark! You can actually hit the target without hitting the bull's-eye, can't you?

We often don't even recognize these "little" sins in our life. Sometimes we just get caught up in the motion of everything around us, and instead of trying to reflect God's holiness, we act like the world around us. Without willfully defying God, we sin. Can you think of some ways that we sometimes miss the bull's-eye but not the target altogether? **Gossip** sure is a great example of this kind of sin, isn't it? I really don't like gossip, and yet sometimes I'm confronted with the fact that by hanging around it, I've condoned it. Worse yet, I sometimes stick in a few jabs myself.

Add a few of your own "little sins" to the target, placing them on the target but not in the bull's-eye.

GOD'S BEST

GOSSIP

Pssstttt . . . and then she said . . .

Now I don't want you to think that God has "levels" of sin and that some of it is okay. It all separates us from Him. It's all sin. I'm just trying

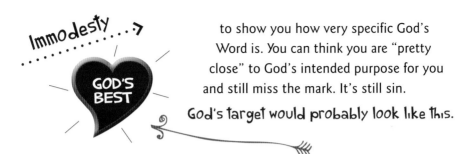

Immodesty ...⇗

GOD'S BEST

to show you how very specific God's Word is. You can think you are "pretty close" to God's intended purpose for you and still miss the mark. It's still sin.

God's target would probably look like this.

I'm wondering, did you include **immodesty** on any of your other targets? I placed it here on this one so it would stick out. (You knew **that** was coming, didn't you?) Can you be living what appears to be a sort of clean life but still miss the mark? Still be sinning? I think you can.

You see, sin isn't just the bad things we do; it's also failing to do the good things. God designed you for good. To be kind and love others and worship Him. And there's one good thing that's more important than all the others.

Time for your power verse.

. . . .

Secret #5 Power Verse
"So, whether you eat or drink, or whatever you do, do all to the glory of God." (I Corinthians 10:31)

. . . .

You were created to glorify God.
Glorify is just a big word that means to make Him known or visible. Kind of like the way the moon makes the sun visible every night. The moon has no light of its own, but it shows off the beauty of the sun every night! In that way, the moon makes the sun known even in the darkness of night. Glorifying God is like that. We make God known even when He can't be seen.

No other purpose is greater than making sure people know and see God in you. And this verse says that anything you do should make people see Him. That includes what you eat, what you drink . . . and what you wear! You were made to cause people to look at God.

The reason immodesty is sin is not because of how short a skirt is or how tight a shirt is. The primary sin of immodesty is that we're saying "look at me" instead of "look at God!"

Secret #5: What we wear becomes sin when it says "look at me" instead of "look at God."

 hat do I mean by that? Well, a lot of times when we reach for a super blingy shirt or an unusually short skirt, it's because we want to say, "Hey, world! Here I am!" There can be a lot of pride and self-focus in the way that we dress. (Of course, sometimes we just really like the dazzly T-shirt and our heart isn't meaning to be the center of attention, and sometimes that is okay.) But if our intention is to say "look at me," it's not okay. It's not appropriate. Because our entire life is meant to glorify God and to say "look at God!"

I really like fashion, but if I dress super crazy when I teach on stage at Secret Keeper Girl, you might have a hard time hearing the Bible verses I'm using to teach you. I don't want the way that I dress to distract from the good work I'm doing to help you see God. Does that make some sense? We say "look at God" best by the good things we do and the gentleness, kindness, and helpfulness we wear on the inside! Remember this power verse from our last chapter?

"I want women to be modest in their appearance. They should wear decent and appropriate clothing and not draw attention to themselves by the way they fix their hair or by wearing gold or pearls or expensive clothes. **For women who claim to be devoted to God should make themselves attractive by the good things they do.**"
(1 Timothy 2:9–10 NLT)

It's the good things we do that should make us attractive, not the awesome clothes we buy! For that reason, when I'm buying clothes— and I really like shopping and fashion—I'm careful to ask myself, "Will this distract people from seeing God in me? Does it say 'look at Dannah' or does it allow my life to say 'look at God'?"

LOOK AT GOD!

Here's another verse that I need to share with you!

> "So whoever knows the
> right thing to do and fails to do it,
> for him it is sin." (James 4:17)

From this day forward, you know the right thing to do. You know that God wants you to dress carefully and modestly so that nothing you wear distracts people from seeing the good things you do so that they can see Jesus in you. Now that you know this: if you fail to do it, it is sin.

Remember, the bull's-eye represents God's intended purpose for your life. His intended purpose for your beauty is to glorify Him—that is, to help people see Him. When we dress modestly so that nothing distracts from the good works we do, people can see God's fingerprint in our internal beauty! When we dress carelessly so that our bodies are the primary focus, people get distracted and can't see inside of us to see God. **So does all this talk about sin sound harsh?** Well, stick with me, because sin is not the most important word in the Bible, and it's not the most important word in this book. That's coming up in the next chapter.

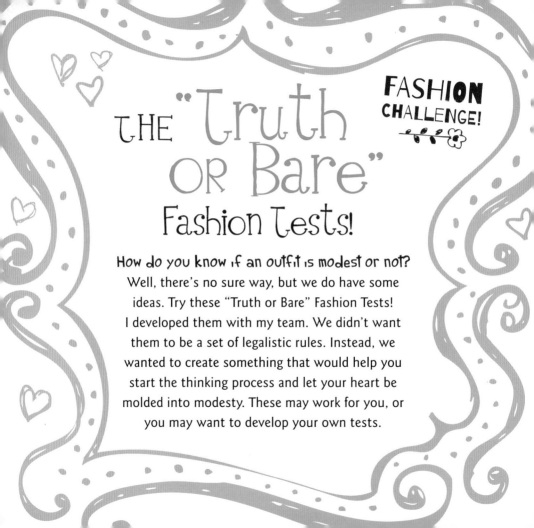

FASHION CHALLENGE!

THE "Truth OR Bare" Fashion Tests!

How do you know if an outfit is modest or not?
Well, there's no sure way, but we do have some
ideas. Try these "Truth or Bare" Fashion Tests!
I developed them with my team. We didn't want
them to be a set of legalistic rules. Instead, we
wanted to create something that would help you
start the thinking process and let your heart be
molded into modesty. These may work for you, or
you may want to develop your own tests.

Raise & Praise

"AM I SHOWING TOO MUCH BELLY?"

Stand and pretend you are totally going for it in worship, lifting your hands in the air with your arms fully extended. Is this exposing any belly skin? Even if you don't raise your hands to worship, just think of all the things you do every day that cause you to lift them.

TEST

1

SOLUTION: Go for layers and put a longer shirt under a shorter one. Our Secret Weapon: a ribbed T-shirt or tank from the boys' or men's department. They're nice and long and stay tucked in under a cool, trendy shirt. No problem here since she's got one under her button-down!

I See London, I See France

TEST
2

"CAN YOU SEE MY UNDERPANTS?"

Bend over and check yourself out in the mirror. (You got it . . . the back view!) Can you see a distinct outline of your panties through your pants, skirt, or shorts? This can happen if your pants are too tight or your undies are too bright!

SOLUTION: Trash your tight pants. For lighter colored pants and skirts, keep a few pairs of "granny panties" (plain white or beige ones) on hand for a safe look.

Mirror Image

"HOW SHORT IS TOO SHORT?"

When you buy either shorts or a skirt, try this test. Sit "criss-cross applesauce" in front of a full-length mirror. What do you see? If you see too much thigh or your panties, guess what? So can everyone else.

TEST

3

SOLUTION: Today's skirts are about extremes. Go for extremely long or extremely full . . . but pass on extremely short. As far as shorts go, longer ones can be hard to find, but keep looking!

The Plumber's Test

TEST 4

"ARE MY PANTS JUST TOO LOW?"
It ain't cute on the plumber, and it ain't cute on girls either. The terrible . . . the awful . . . crack view! Sit cross-legged on the floor. Bend forward as if you're about to devour a great magazine. Now, reach behind you and get a feel of what might be the featured view if your jeans are too low. (Or ask a girlfriend to check it out!)

SOLUTION: Time to reach for that Secret Weapon again: a guy's tank or T-shirt. And always be willing to consider that some low riders are just too low. Find a pair that won't cause viewers to blush.

Stand In The Gap

"TELL ME NOW . . . IS MY SHIRT TOO TIGHT?"
When wearing a button-down shirt, stand sideways
and look in the mirror. Is the space between the buttons
gaping open, even just a little bit? If it's pulling enough
to cause a gap, you're in danger of exposing way too
much and in danger of losing a button!

SOLUTION: It's a no-brainer. Too-tight shirts are a
totally bad idea if you want to dress modestly. It's
not JUST about how much of your beautiful epidermis
is showing, but how much of your shape is showing!
Try buying a size or two larger. (If that bugs you, cut
out the tag when you get home.) Or try a shirt under
the button-down, and leave the shirt unbuttoned
for a layered look.

TEST
5

Palm Pilot

"IS MY SHIRT TOO LOW?"

How do you know if your shirt is too low? Well, take your hand and hook your thumb onto that little shelf under your neck. (That's your collarbone. Feel around. You'll find it.) Now, lay your palm nice and flat on your chest so the pinkie is about 5-6 inches under the thumb. Is there any skin showing below your pinkie? If so, you really need to think about this shirt.

SOLUTION: Guess what? Our Secret Weapon works for low shirts as well as short shirts! You can also try a trendy layering technique by putting a button-down under a polo or rugby shirt that plunges too low.

THE **SECRET** Weapon

Grab a few of these in the boys' or men's department. **Simple tank T's.** They're great wardrobe lifesavers. Why the men's department? Because they make men's shirts nice and long and you'll have lots to tuck into your pants or keep long for the layered look.

Keep your eyes open. I find tanks of varying colors that are nice and long at some of my favorite stores just for girls! Once you have a collection, you'll always have a great modest and trendy fashion solution on hand!

The Bottom Line

[If you love God, you will obey Him in the way you dress.]

Is it my fault I can play ball better than most boys?
No! But my dad is so obsessed with what I wear when I

...protecting his "wittle girl."

play with them, that he can't even see
my mad skills. Grrrrrr! Today before
he would drive me to practice, he made
me go back to my room and change.
TWICE. He said my pants were too
tight. Too tight for what, running
around the bases? Sitting on the bench to wait my
turn? Knocking the ball outta the park? Dad says he's
just protecting his "wittle girl." Oh brother! I feel
half crazy because I don't want to need protecting.

On the other hand, when I thought about it I really do trust my dad even though I don't understand what he's thinking! Yeah, I love him. So, I'll stick with sweatpants when I play ball with the boys. -Toni

Do you find all this modesty stuff hard to swallow? Have I ruffled your feathers? Would you rather not know these simple truths I've taught you because it means you have to either reject or embrace them? I understand. They can be a pain in the neck, and some people get so uptight about fashion. I assure you that if I saw you looking absolutely adorable in something trendy, I would say "You look adorbs!" I like fashion, but I love Jesus! And I want to make sure my life shines for Him. So, I have embraced the Bible's teaching on beauty and fashion. **AND MODESTY!**

I remember a time in sixth grade when my dad didn't like my shoes. **My shoes!** My Nana gave me those shoes when she didn't want to wear them anymore. They were royal blue fabric heels. They were better for dancing than for doing math, but my dad said they were "boy catcher" shoes. (He had a way of being extreme sometimes when it came to protecting me.) They said, "Here I am! Look at me!" They did not say, "Look at God!"

I was dressed for school and running to catch my bus when my dad noticed me. He calmly pulled the newspaper away from his face and said, "You need to change your shoes into something sensible before you leave for school."

And then he put his newspaper back up.

"Daaaaddddd! I'll miss the school bus." I whined.

As calmly as he could, my dad simply said, "Then, prepare to walk to school!"

Of course, he didn't really mean it. My school was 20 miles away from my house, but his message was clear: you're changing your shoes one way or another.

I am afraid I didn't act as if I loved my dad that day, and for that I'm sorry. I pouted and stomped out the door in my boring flats. Now I realize that my dad was just protecting me because he **LOVED ME!**

WOW!

Think about it. When your mom and dad put boundaries on the things you do, they are really saying, "I love you."

💜 **WHEN** they don't let you play in the street when you're a toddler, it's because they love you and don't want you to get hit by a car.

💜 **WHEN** they don't let you eat ice cream before you eat veggies, it's because they love you and don't want your body to be addicted to sugar.

💜 **WHEN** they don't let you go to a movie that's not okay, it's because they love you and don't want you to have images in your head that you can't get out.

💜 **WHEN** they don't let you wear a super short skirt to school, it's because they love you and want people to see the brains and beauty **INSIDE** of you and not to get stuck on the outside stuff.

OK now that we have established that rules mean your parents love you, let's imagine every time your mom or dad says "no" you can actually hear them saying, "I love you!" (Of course, you're going to have to listen real hard to hear that, I'm sure. But play along!)

What do you say when someone you love says, "I love you"?

You say, "I love you" back!

How do you say that when the way they say "I love you" is putting boundaries on your behavior? You obey them! And you do it with a good heart!

Let me be honest with you. If you don't like what you're reading in this book or are planning to ignore it, you probably don't have a modesty problem. *You have a love problem.*

You see, sin is not the most important word in the Bible. **LOVE** is.

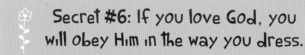

Secret #6: If you love God, you will obey Him in the way you dress.

You see, when you truly love God, you obey Him. His guidelines for living may still be hard to swallow, but you still follow them because you realize it's about *loving Him.*

. . . .

Secret #6 Power Verse
*"Whoever has my commandments and keeps them,
he it is who loves me. And he who loves me
will be loved by my Father, and I will love him
and manifest myself to him." (John 14:21)*

. . . .

If you are struggling to obey God in the area of modesty, maybe it's just because you and I can be really stubborn sometimes when it comes to obeying God. But maybe it's because you do not really know Him and His deep love for you. It's easy to know about God and His Son. Lots of people do. But few actually, really intimately know Him. And when you do truly know Him, you can't help but love Him.

DO YOU LOVE HIM? 💜 HE SURE LOVES YOU!

How do I know? Because the way He has responded to your sin and mine is so radically, crazy full of love. It's normal to get in trouble when you do something wrong. Once I talked back to my dad and got grounded for a week. No parties. No TV. No friends. No soccer practice. Nothing! I was in my room doing homework or doing chores when I wasn't at school. I deserved that punishment. It was normal for my mom and dad to react that way. And in that case, normal was good.

But God isn't normal. And He doesn't treat us normally either. He doesn't treat us the way we *deserve* to be treated! Psalm 103:9–10 says, "He never bears a grudge, nor remains angry forever. He has not punished us as we deserve for all our sins" (TLB).

Don't get me wrong. God handed out a punishment for your sins.

🦋 That lie you told . . .

🦋 The mean thing you said to a classmate . . .

🦋 The sass you gave your mom last week . . .

Those sins did not go unpunished.

But you weren't the one who had to take the punishment. And the punishment was real, real harsh! Romans 6:23 says the punishment for sin is *death*!

[BUT!]

Our God is not normal. He loves like **CRAZY!!** Romans 6:23 in all of its glory reads: "The wages of sin is death, but the free gift of God is eternal life in Christ Jesus our Lord"! So if you didn't have to pay the penalty for your sin, who did? Jesus did! Isaiah 53 says God put

on Him all the weight of our sin. Jesus paid it all. He went to the cross carrying every one of our sins upon His back—our lying, our meanness, our disobedience—and He paid it all for you and for me **BECAUSE HE LOVES US!** He wanted to give us the free gift of forgiveness and eternal life.

The only thing we have to do is accept His free gift, and when we do, it's kind of like being adopted into this family. Because we become a part of the family of God.

I adopted my daughter Autumn when she was 13 years old. It was one of the best days of my life. You know, when we adopted her, she had to go in front of a judge and testify that she *wanted* to be adopted. Coming into God's family is a little like that. You have to **CHOOSE IT**. I'm wondering if you've ever done that? Do you

remember a time when you did?

If you don't, put this book down and talk to your mom right now and ask her! (Come back after you and her have a good talk.)

If you do, keep reading!

Make no mistake. It is God who desires for you to dress modestly and reveal your inner beauty by protecting you with modesty. When we love Him, this comes a tad more naturally. Don't try to just dress how God wants you to dress unless you first have been adopted into His family and entered into His LOVE!

If Jesus were to write you a love note, I think this might be what it would say. I got the truths in most of the sentences in this love note from verses in the Bible. I just rewrote them directly to you.

My Precious Masterpiece,

Have the bad-hair days and expensive brand-name jeans your mom won't buy you gotten the worst of you? Oh, if only you could see how brilliant a masterpiece you are.

I couldn't wait for you to arrive. You! Yes, you! I've anticipated your presence on My earth before it was even created.

Like a master embroiderer sits at his loom painstakingly interweaving each unique strand, I knit you together piece by piece with intention and precision. You are one of the unique expressions of My own glory. I chose the color of your hair from the earth and the color of your eyes from the beauty of My creation. I even placed My thumb there on your nose, marking it with My fingerprint.

After you were made in secret, I revealed you to this world, with still the most profound parts of your beauty waiting to be crafted. Still, I am creating you in secret, My masterpiece.

Though the full secrets of your beauty are unknown to the world, I see. And I am enthralled by your beauty.

Oh, how I love you.

There have been only a few places on earth that I have been willing to fill with My own radiant glory—the tabernacle, the old temple . . . and you! That's how precious your body is to Me.

Will you honor Me with it?

Will you love Me back?

Your Master Craftsman, Jesus*

*This letter from Jesus is written using Ephesians 1:4–7; Psalm 139:13–16; Psalm 45:11–14; 1 Corinthians 6:19–20.

DO YOU LOVE HIM?

{
*"Or do you not know that your body is a
temple of the Holy Spirit within you,
whom you have from God? You are not your own,
for you were bought with a price.
So glorify God in your body."*
(1 Corinthians 6:19–20)
}

Finding True Beauty

[The source of true beauty is a love relationship with Jesus!]

...maybe even ... pretty!

Dear God, I've been writing in this journal a whole lot and noticed something. Sometimes I write to You. Sometimes I just write. Without a doubt the times I write to You, I feel better. I mean, it's cool to write about Zachary Donaldson appearances and who got picked first in gym class, but where does it get me? Usually, just more frustrated. But when I write to You, I feel peaceful. Happy. Maybe even ... pretty! So, I dedicate this diary to talking to You! From this day to forever! —Danika

I can't let you go without telling you how to get true beauty! Just where does it really come from? I mean, we know it's not something you can buy at the mall. Wouldn't it be easier if there were a True Beauty Mall? Can you imagine the beautiful inner shoes for your feet to carry the love of Jesus to other people that could be found at Pay-It-Forward Shoes? And, oh, the jewels for your heart like earrings of grace, and chokers of self-control, and bracelets of joy to be found at Clara's Inner Beauty Jewelry Boutique? And the garments that get us geared up to do good works at Justice Good Deeds Duds? (Did you see what I did there? I tried to use the names of famous name brands with a twist. I crack myself up!)

WHAT?!

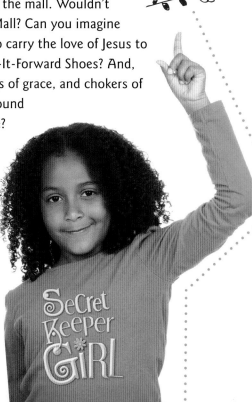

Okay, there is no True Beauty Mall.

So, I'm going to tell you where to go to get true beauty. But first, let's review the six secrets we learned in the first six chapters of this book. (By the way, good job making it this far. This is really a self-help book and lots of girls aren't ready for them until high school, but I'm proud of you for devouring this one!)

[REVIEW OF TRUE BEAUTY SECRETS!]

1. You are a masterpiece created by God.

2. True beauty doesn't come from what's on the outside.

3. True beauty is not about how you look. It's about how you see.

4. God wants nothing we wear to distract people from seeing our true beauty.

5. What we wear becomes sin when it says "look at me" instead of "look at God."

6. If you love God, you will obey Him in the way you dress.

Now, it's time for **Secret #7**, which tells us where to get true beauty. The fact is, you *can* "get" it somewhere.

I got it and when I did, I didn't hate what I saw when I looked in the mirror. And trust me, I used to hate it so much that I would **not** look in the mirror. This started in my tweens and lasted all the way through my college years. I actually learned how to put mascara on without looking in the mirror because I disliked what I saw there so very much . . . until I found the Source of true beauty. Now I actually like what I see. It's not like I look in the mirror and say, "Wow, girl! You

WHAT HE MADE IS GOOD!

are one gorgeous chick!" No, I just kind of look in the mirror and know I'm a masterpiece created by God and think one very simple thought: "What He made is good." Oh, it gives me butterflies in my tummy right now as I write this and think of you finding that.

I've been helping girls find it ever since I started Secret Keeper Girl in 2003. That's a lot of years ago. (You weren't even born yet!) So I really love helping girls experience God and His Presence.

About 350,000 girls and moms have attended one of my live Secret Keeper Girl events, where I teach them how to find the Source of true beauty. God is bringing to my mind some girls who found it.

Here is what girls have experienced when they use this last secret **FAITHFULLY**

They begin to think insanely GREAT things about being a masterpiece created by God, and I **DO** want *you* to think these things!

One girl in Canada who always used bulky, oversized clothes to cover herself up and hide her body began to think that she was actually quite beautiful. She began working out and wearing clothes that were modest but never failed to be super cute. *She began to think that she was a masterpiece created by God.* **(DO that!)**

One girl in Pittsburgh, Pennsylvania, who had to have a lot of corrective surgeries on her teeth and jaws began to see all those painful experiences as a way God was giving her more than just beautiful teeth. She began to think He was giving her "heart" surgery so she could learn patience, perseverance, and courage. *She began to think that God had purpose in her physical suffering.* **(DO that!)**

One girl in Jarabacoa, Dominican Republic, who disliked herself so badly that she was doing terrible things to physically change her body, stopped hurting herself. She began to think that God made her right after all and started to have contentment and gratitude for how she was created. *She began to think she should teach other girls that they were just right the way they were created, too.* **(DO that!)**

One girl in California who dressed in super-tight clothes and super-short shorts and super-low-cut shirts threw them all away one day. She asked her mom to take her to the Goodwill store to buy "new" vintagey clothes because she wanted to dress modestly. No one told her to do that. *She began to think she could choose to obey God.* (DO that!)

Here's the thing: the secret I'm about to teach you **works**.

It's been proven over and over again that what I'm about to tell you to do will make you feel better about yourself. In fact, I've never heard from one girl or woman who did what I'm going to ask of you who didn't feel better about herself after the time was up. (It's gonna take a bit to let it all sink in.)

It's important to return to something I said before: feelings aren't facts. But when we base what we feel on facts and feel better about something because it's truth, it's good! It's good to have good feelings because you have found truthful facts to live by.

Using God's standard and His way of finding true beauty to make you feel better about yourself is like drinking refreshing water from a huge fire hose. You'll never even be able to drink all of what He has to give you.

IT'S NOT ALWAYS EASY!

I know that this secret—more than all the others—can make you feel confident and aaamazing, **IF YOU DO WHAT I ASK OF YOU!**

There's the rub! This isn't going to come easy. It's not for the girl who can't roll up her sleeves and do a little hard stuff. I have found that I have to be **FAITHFUL** to get into God's Word and do a lot of hard stuff in order to feel His presence. What kind of hard stuff? Like getting up early to read the Bible. Or staying up late. Or saying "no" when a friend wants to hang out because I know I need to spend some time praying. It's not always easy. But it's always rewarding. It makes me feel more confident. And the sense of God's presence is aaamazing!.

Do you want to feel confident and aaamazing?

Read on!

Take a look at this power verse, which we used earlier in the book.

"Your beauty should not come from outward adornment, such as elaborate hairstyles and the wearing of gold jewelry or fine clothes. Rather, it should be that of your inner self, the unfading beauty of a gentle and quiet spirit, which is of great worth in God's sight." (I Peter 3:3–4 NIV)

When do you get a gentle and quiet spirit? You get it when your inner self is made beautiful by a love relationship with Jesus.

Secret #7: The source of true beauty is a love relationship with Jesus!

What 1 Peter 3:3–4 is really challenging is this: "Do you spend more time in front of the mirror making yourself externally beautiful, or do you spend more time developing your inner beauty through quiet communion with God?"

Secret #7 Power Verse

"You shall love the LORD your God with all your heart and with all your soul and with all your might."

(Deuteronomy 6:5)

It takes **STRENGTH** to love God. All of our STRENGTH! That means you put effort into it, and that's what I'd like to encourage you to do. I'd like to ask you to take my Secret Keeper Girl **True Beauty Challenge**. Here's how it works:

Challenge yourself each day to spend a little more time with God than you spend working on your external self. If your morning beauty routine is fifteen minutes, try for twenty minutes of time alone with God. Although I don't want you to get caught up in watching the clock, I know that pushing yourself in this area of discipline will change you immensely. Let me say this one more time: it's not about watching the clock but taking care to be more concerned with grooming your heart than your face. Make sense?

I want you to do this for the next seven weeks, for five out of seven days a week. **WHOA!** That sounds like a big investment of time, doesn't it? Well, I've been doing it for twenty-three **YEARS!** Do you know what's happened? I've changed from a girl who disliked what I saw in the mirror so much that I would not look in it to a woman who looks in the mirror and thinks, "I'm a masterpiece created by God!"

Working on my internal beauty has helped me to accept my external beauty. And I like spending time increasing my love relationship with Jesus so much that I keep doing it year after year, month after month, day after day. You might like it that much, too. But I'm only asking you to do it for **SEVEN WEEKS!** Why seven weeks? Because they say it takes forty days to develop a habit, and I want spending time in God's presence to become a habit for you.

A lot of people will say I'm crazy for asking you. (*That's not what God says.* He says we should start EVERY DAY with prayer. That's Psalm 119:147.)

Some people will say you are too young. (*That is not what God says.* He says "Don't let anyone look down on you because you are young, but set an example for the believers in speech, in conduct, in love, in faith and in purity." That's 1 Timothy 4:12 NIV.)

Some people will say there are better things to do with your time. No way! There's no better use of your time than spending it on Jesus! In fact, it says He's supposed to be the FIRST thing that we spend time on (Matthew 6:33). You can do this. I would not be asking this big thing from you if I didn't believe that you could do it.

Ask your mom to join you in the challenge. It helps a lot to have someone doing it with you. You can agree to the challenge by signing the True Beauty Challenge on the next page. After you both sign it, tear it out and tape it to your bathroom mirror.

C Every day, before you officially start your day, spend time reading God's Word and praying on your own. Once a week, check in with your mom.

A really great tool to use during these seven weeks is the *Secret Keeper Girl Mom-Daughter Devos with Coloring Experience*. I wrote it just for this *Secret Keeper Girl True Beauty Challenge*. It has devotions written for you to use five days a week, and the last one of the week is a coloring experience for you and your mom. You can color while you talk about the lessons you've learned.

Of course, you can do this without the *Secret Keeper Girl Mom-Daughter Devos with Coloring Experience* by using your own devotional tools or even just the Bible and a journal.

Or, you could go to secretkeepergirl.com and sign up for my **FREE Ten-Day True Beauty Challenge**. You'll find it on the home page. These ten devotions on true beauty would get you started, so the first two weeks would be all ready to go!

No matter how you approach it, every day I want you to ask yourself the question:

{ "Today, did I spend more time in God's Word or in front of this mirror?" }

Are you ready to dive in?
If so, **Sign** the True Beauty Challenge. And **dive in!**

Dannah Gresh's Secret Keeper Girl

TRUE BEAUTY CHALLENGE:

{ "Today, did I spend more time in God's Word or in front of this mirror?" }

"Your beauty should not come from outward adornment, such as elaborate hairstyles and the wearing of gold jewelry or fine clothes. Rather, it should be that of your inner self, the unfading beauty of a gentle and quiet spirit, which is of great worth in God's sight." (1 Peter 3:3–4 NIV)

We, _____ and

_____, will attempt to

spend_____ and_____minutes a day in quiet

prayer and Bible reading during the next seven weeks.

We commit to do this for five out of every seven days.

Signed:_____

Date: _____

Signed:_____

Date: _____

The Secret Keeper Girl True Beauty Challenge is a creation of Dannah Gresh, as published in *Secret Keeper Girl: The Power of Modesty for Tweens* by Moody Publishers. To learn more, go to secretkeepergirl.com.

APPENDIX

The Secrets of True Beauty for Every Secret Keeper Girl

(And the power verses you need!)

1 **You are a masterpiece created by God.** "I praise you, for I am fearfully and wonderfully made. Wonderful are your works; my soul knows it very well. My frame was not hidden from you, when I was being made in secret, intricately woven . . ." Psalm 139:14–15

2 **True beauty doesn't come from what's on the outside.** "Your beauty should not come from outward adornment, such as elaborate hairstyles and the wearing of gold jewelry or fine clothes." 1 Peter 3:3 (NIV)

3 **True beauty is not about how you look. It's about how you see.** "Be beautiful inside, in your hearts, with the lasting charm of a gentle and quiet spirit that is so precious to God." 1 Peter 3:4 (TLB)

4 God wants nothing we wear to distract people from seeing our true beauty. "I want women to be modest in their appearance. They should wear decent and appropriate clothing and not draw attention to themselves by the way they fix their hair or by wearing gold or pearls or expensive clothes. For women who claim to be devoted to God should make themselves attractive by the good things they do." 1 Timothy 2:9–10 (NLT)

5 What we wear becomes sin when it says "look at me" instead of "look at God." "So whoever knows the right thing to do and fails to do it, for him it is sin." James 4:17

6 If you love God, you will obey Him in the way you dress. "Whoever has my commandments and keeps them, he it is who loves me. And he who loves me will be loved by my Father, and I will love him and manifest myself to him." John 14:21

7 The source of true beauty is a love relationship with Jesus! "You shall love the LORD your God with all your heart and with all your soul and with all your might." Deuteronomy 6:5

NOTES

1. "secret," definition #11, http://www.dictionary.com/browse/secret.

2. Girls aged 8–12 spend about $500 million per year on beauty products alone! Deborah Swaney, "Fast Times: When did 7 become the new 16?" *Family Circle,* November 29, 2008, 48.

3. According to one Harvard study, two-thirds of underweight twelve-year-olds considered themselves fat, 80% of ten year olds have been on a diet, and 34% cut back on their eating without telling mom. *Good Housekeeping,* August 1, 2006.

4. This thought about being a coward or having courage is from the introduction in C. S. Lewis's *Mere Christianity.* It's not an original thought.

5. "counterfeit," definition #3, http://www.dictionary.com/browse/counterfeit.

6. This text and some other material was adapted from text originally published in my book *Secret Keeper: The Delicate Power of Modesty* (Chicago: Moody, 2002).

7. "curator," definition #1, http://www.dictionary.com/browse/curator.

This book gets even better when you use its companion!

Secret Keeper Girl: Mom-Daughter Devos
with Coloring Experience
DANNAH GRESH

ACKNOWLEDGMENTS

I would like to thank all of you who helped in one way or another for your contribution to my book.

First and foremost, I would like to thank my good friend Joe Weseling for his six, hand-drawn illustrations. Due to time constraints, he was unable to complete the seventh. I would like to thank my cousin Lisa Timoteo for stepping in and drawing the seventh one which is the new referee's position.

Many friends read my manuscript to help make sure the spelling, punctuation, sentence structure, and paragraph breaks were all correct. This includes Joan Bresnicky and her husband Jim, Larry Nelson, Celeste Wiggins, and Jerry and Diane Karp. Thank you all for taking the time to help. Thanks to Mike Papouras who acted as my technical advisor and made sure my descriptions of wrestling maneuvers and rules were precise.

Thank you to David, Leah, and Zak, my middle grade readers who answered questions about interest and grade appropriateness.

Last, but certainly not least, I would like to thank the team from Createspace for their help in bringing my book to the market place in excellent condition.

"Ready, Wrestle"

By Bob Timoteo

Chapter 1

John Lester and Bill Thomas were great friends. They lived next door to each other and did many things together. Bill was one grade ahead of John at Claremont High School. John was a freshman and Bill was a sophomore.

John was smaller in height and weight than his friend Bill. However, that did not stop them from a friendly session of wrestling together in Bill's family's carpeted recreation room from time to time.

One day, on the way to school, John was more quiet than usual and Bill asked, "What's wrong?"

John said, "I'm upset because I wanted to try out for football in the fall and the head football coach, Mr. Johnson, said that he felt I was too small and might get injured. I had already taken my physical in the hope that

I would have a chance to be on the team." John continued, "He then suggested that I become one of the team managers. You know, passing out equipment and making sure the medical kits are up to date with bandages and other first aid equipment. I also had to make sure the water bottles were full before we went out to the prac-tice field. While all of this is important, I'd prefer to have had the opportunity to play.

"I recently stopped in to see the basketball coach, and after looking me over, he sug-gested that I should do the same thing for his team. I know I'm short right now, but by the time I get to my junior year, I might be big enough to play at point guard. I love sports so much and yet I have not been able to participate on any of the school teams."

Bill felt sorry for John and said he had a great idea. "Why don't you go and talk to Mr. Smith, the wrestling coach? He's always looking for additional people to wrestle for the team. You know, there are many weight classes and I'm sure you'll be able to wres-tle at 106 pounds."

That day, after school, John went down to the wrestling room to talk with Coach Smith. Coach Smith saw John come into the wrestling room and approached him. "Hi there, young man, I'm Coach Smith, the head wrestling coach here at Claremont. What can I do for you?"

"Coach Smith, it's a pleasure to meet you. I'm John Lester and my best friend, Bill Thomas, is a member of your team. I love sports, but as you can see, I'm pretty small. Bill thought I'd fit right in at 106 pounds."

"Well, John," said Coach Smith, "let's put you on the scale and find out how much you weigh." They went over to the large scale in the corner of the wrestling room and John got on. With all of his clothes on, he weighed in at 104 pounds.

Coach Smith seemed extremely happy and said to John, "I need a 106-pound wrestler to fill out the team roster. You would fit in perfectly. In fact, the way you are dressed means your actual weight is probably about 102 pounds or so. I am sure you would have no trouble making weight for all of the matches."

Coach Smith asked John if he knew anything about wrestling. John answered by telling him how he and Bill Thomas often wrestled in Bill's recreation room, and that Bill had shown him several really great moves. "Depending on how much you grow in the next year, I'd guess you might be able to wrestle at 106 pounds next year too. You probably will get taller, but you might not put on too much weight between now and then."

"John," continued the coach, "are you a good student? You know it's very important that athletes have good grades so that they can remain eligible for all the matches and games in which they play!"

"Don't worry," said John, "I'm a B+ student, and I enjoy writing, reading, and math."

Coach Smith seemed pleased with John's answers. "Then all you have to do now is get a permission slip signed by your parents, take a physical, and the hydration and percentage of body fat tests."

John said that he had already taken a physical exam when he thought he was going to try out for the football team.

"Great, then you'll be able to start working out next week once your parents sign your slip."

"That won't be a problem," John said. "They know I want to participate in sports."

"Good, I'll set it up for the trainer to give you the hydration and percentage of body fat tests before you come to practice."

A few minutes later, the team started to arrive dressed in their practice gear.

When Bill saw John there, he ran up to him and asked, "John, what did Coach Smith say?"

John smiled from ear to ear and said, "The coach told me I could start Monday once my parents sign my permission slip and I have the two necessary tests."

"Do you think you'll have any problem with them signing your permission slip?" Bill asked.

"No, they know how much I want to participate in sports. They really want me to participate in extracurricular activities and wrestling seems to be the perfect sport for me due to the many weight classes."

Coach Smith told John that he could stay and watch the practice session if he wanted to. He said it would be just fine if he thought his parents would not mind him coming home a little late from school.

John said, "I'm sure it will be okay, because as the football manager, I regularly got home later anyway."

When practice was over, and Bill was finished showering, he and John ran all the way home to talk with John's parents.

They ran into the house and John yelled, "Mom, Dad, where are you? I have great news."

Mr. and Mrs. Lester hurried from the kitchen where Mrs. Lester had been preparing dinner and talking to Mr. Lester about the busy day they each had. "John, what's all the excitement about? We haven't seen you this excited since we went to the Grand Canyon on our last vacation," his dad said.

"Mom, Dad, I'm so excited. You know how much I love sports, and how I've been trying to participate in high school."

"Yes," they both replied with some degree of excitement in their voices, seeming to catch the enthusiasm of their son and his best friend.

"Well, Bill is on the wrestling team at school and was last year as well. He suggested I talk to the wrestling coach, Mr. Smith, and I did that after school today. He weighed me and asked me to stay and watch practice so I could see some of the moves and holds

"Ready, Wrestle"

I would need to learn when I start practicing with the team. I just need you to sign
my permission slip and I can start Monday.
Please, please say you'll sign it for me. You
know how much I love sports."

"How can you wrestle for the team?" asked
John's dad. "You are only a freshman and
you are also very small for your age."

"Oh, that's another great thing," said Bill.
"Ninth graders are eligible to wrestle varsity
in Ohio, if they are good enough. You may
not remember, but I wrestled varsity last
year when I was only in the ninth grade. I
think John would be really good. We wrestle all the time in our recreation room, and I
have a very difficult time beating him even
though I know a lot more about wrestling
than he does. He is pretty strong for his size."

John added, "As far as my size is concerned, there are fourteen weight classes.
I would only be wrestling against boys in
my weight class. I would be able to wrestle
at 106 pounds. Coach Smith thought that
I would be perfect at that weight, and at

the present time, I would be the only person able to make weight at 106 pounds."

John's dad asked, "Where's your permission slip? I'll sign it right now." John pulled it out of his book bag and his dad signed it immediately.

John then told his mom and dad that he would need wrestling shoes and headgear and some other wrestling equipment before Monday. He then asked, "May we go to the sporting goods store on Saturday to purchase them?"

They smiled and said, "Yes." They were very happy for their son.

Then John and Bill ran out of the house and went next door to tell Bill's parents the great news. That night, John could hardly sleep knowing that on Monday he was finally going to be a part of a sports team at his high school. He would be starting out on a new and wonderful adventure.

Chapter 2

On Saturday morning, John was up bright and early to go shopping for his equipment. When he came down to the kitchen, he was happy to see that both of his parents were awake and seemed anxious to go shopping too. They asked John if he would like Bill to come along. John was only too happy to have his best friend along and asked if they could then go out to breakfast. His parents smiled and said, "Okay."

They arrived at the mall shortly after the stores opened for the day, and went directly to the sporting goods store. The store was the one recommended by the school for all of its teams' equipment, so getting the right colors for the shoes and headgear was not a problem.

Bill suggested to John's parents that they also purchase matching kneepads and a singlet, the thigh length outfit used for practice sessions. He said the school supplied the team singlet and warm-ups used for matches, but all of the boys had to provide their own practice gear. The school's colors are red and white and the sporting goods store had plenty of equipment on hand in those colors.

John bought a red singlet, a red and white headgear, red kneepads, and white shoes. Bill told him all of the wrestlers had the same colors. When they left the store, John felt he was ready for anything now.

All four of them went to Bernie's Breakfast Hut and the boys ate a huge meal. John's dad said, "If you two continue to eat like you just did, neither of you will be able to make weight this season."

The boys both laughed and Bill said, "We don't always eat this way, but we get extra pounds as the season goes on."

Bill went on to explain that John would have to have two tests done that all the other wrestlers had already taken. He said, "The first one is a hydration test, and the second one is a test that measures the percentage of body fat each of us have. These two tests determine the lowest weight class where each of us can wrestle. No one can go below that weight. This keeps wrestlers from trying to go to a weight class that puts them in danger of damaging their health."

John's mom asked what they had to do for John to have these two tests.

Bill explained that the school's team trainer was certified by the state to administer both of these tests. He said he could have them done during a free period or just before practice started Monday.

He then told them that just prior to the start of the season the coaches would hold an evening practice and ask the parents of all of the wrestlers to attend. As part of that practice, he would show them some wrestling maneuvers, explain the basic rules, and show them how the match scoring is done.

"He will also explain that the state rules allow for the natural growth of the wrestlers. They do this by adding weight to each class as the season progresses. On Christmas Day, each wrestler gets two pounds added to his weight class. We also get an extra pound on the second day of a two day tournament."

They left the restaurant and headed home. The boys were very anxious for Monday to come so they could get to practice. In order to burn off some of their energy when they arrived at home, they both changed clothes and went out for a run. Bill said to John, "We do a lot of running before and after practice. Coach Smith believes that being in better condition than our opponents is the key to success on the wrestling mat."

Although John never said anything to Bill about it, when they were finished with their run on Saturday, he had tried on all of his new equipment to see how he looked. He thought he looked pretty cool in his new practice uniform.

Chapter 3

According to the Ohio High School Athletic Association, wrestling practice could not begin until the second Monday of November. John had only missed one week of practice up to that point. He felt that it would not take him too long to catch up to the other newer wrestlers. Much of what had been shown so far was review for the boys who had wrestled in previous years. John knew some of it because Bill had shown him so many things when they wrestled in his basement.

When classes were over on Monday, John and Bill headed to the locker room to change into their practice gear. Then they went into the wrestling room and began some light rolling around just to loosen up a little.

As more and more of the other wrestlers arrived, Bill introduced John to some of the boys he did not know. He already knew most of the freshmen because they had a lot of classes together. He also knew several of the upper classmen because they played on the football team and he had been one of the team managers.

They were all very happy to see him because it meant that they now had all fourteen weight classes filled on the Varsity team, and they would not have to forfeit any weight classes to their opponents. John could hardly wait to get started since he was finally going to get a chance to compete for a school team.

Bill told John that the coaches always started and ended the practice sessions by having the boys run ten laps around the wrestling room. Once they completed the first ten laps, Coach Smith blew his whistle and got them organized for calisthenics.

He again welcomed John to the team and introduced him to the other two coaches, Coach Benson and Coach Collona. After some jumping jacks and some stretching exercises, the coaches put the team through a rigorous routine of wrestling-related moves to help loosen them up even more.

After practice, while the boys were running their ten laps around the wrestling room, the coaches got together to discuss what had taken place. Coach Smith said to his two assistants, "I was very surprised and happy to see how well John Lester did at his first practice." Both coaches agreed with him wholeheartedly.

Coach Benson said, "It shows that he had indeed learned a lot of wrestling by going against Bill in his recreation room at home."

Coach Collona said, "Just watching the way John moves on the mat shows me that he might be a natural athlete even though he is small."

They reminded all of the boys to do their homework and to get plenty of rest so they would be ready for classes in the morning. They also told some of the boys, who were very close to their wrestling weight, to eat a good balanced meal, and to avoid overeating.

John could hardly wait to get home and tell his parents what a terrific time he had at his first practice. His mood was very upbeat while he explained everything that had happened to him. They were very happy that he had been able to fit in so well.

He explained to his parents how technical and intense practice had been. He said, "What Bill and I were doing when we wrestled in his recreation room was good, but not nearly as exciting as actually learning more about all phases of wrestling."

He said to them, "The coaches all thought that I performed well and that I seemed to be catching on to things quickly." He continued, "The coaches were very complimentary to me, considering this was my first official practice session."

He also said, "I was able to take down one of the other freshmen who would probably be the junior varsity 113-pound wrestler. I was almost pinned by an eleventh grader who will probably be the varsity 120-pound starter. I was able to fight off of my back to keep from getting pinned."

His mom and dad seemed really excited for him and were happy to hear about his first day on the mats. They both said almost at the same time, "Tell us more about what else happened at practice." John was only too happy to continue telling them about his practice session.

"Practice usually begins with the main emphasis on conditioning. Then they have us review what was introduced to us the day before. They spend quite a bit of time practicing yesterday's moves and then they introduce us to more new moves. Of course, most of them were new to me."

John continued talking about what was going on. "Over the last summer vacation, a new weight room was added onto the gym building. All of us are encouraged to work out in the weight room during a free period, as long as our grades are in good shape."

He also explained that there were going to be some sessions during the regular wrestling practices when the whole team would spend practice time in the weight room. "Coach Collona is in charge of the weight room as part of his duties at the school. He also teaches physical education and health classes and is going to be the new head football coach next season. Everyone knows that Coach Johnson, the current head coach, is going to retire from teaching and coaching altogether after this year."

Chapter 4

After John's second day of practice, his mood was very upbeat when he got home. He went up to his room and began doing some of his homework. He had been doing homework for about an hour when his mom called up that dinner was ready. He put away his books and hurried downstairs.

He said, "Mom, I'm very hungry and am glad that dinner is ready a little earlier than usual." When they sat down to dinner, his parents asked him how his second day of practice had gone. "I'm glad you asked, because I could hardly wait to tell you all about it.

"We started out doing our normal warm-up routine of ten laps around the room, some light exercises, and then stretching. Then they had us get into the referee's position on the mat with both hands and knees on the mat. All of us did the same drills at the same time. We were not working in pairs during this drill. Then one of the coaches blows his whistle and we have to stand up and reach to our stomachs as though we were pulling our opponent's hand off of our stomachs in an escape attempt. We did this several times, and had to do it to both the left and right sides of our bodies. We do this because our opponents can line up on either side of us in the referee's position during a real match. They want us to be able to work against our opponent, no matter which side he chooses."

He told them the next drill was also in the referee's position on the mat, but we worked in pairs for this one. "In this drill, the boy in the top position tries to break down his partner's stance. We do this by moving our arm from around his waist to the far ankle, and then lift the ankle into the air and push forward using our legs for momentum. At the same time, we move the hand that was on his elbow, to the bottom boy's waist." John then got up from the table and demonstrated the move so they could see how quickly it had to be done.

"We practiced this several times on both the left and then right side of our partner. We do this to break down the bottom boy's base and put him flat on the mat. Then we switched positions and became the bottom boy so our partner could work on the same move.

"We continued doing these and other wrestling moves as part of the normal warm-up routine. The coaches explained to us that wrestling moves have to become natural. Wrestlers must learn to go from one move to the next, to the next, in a series of quick moves. They said that if we have to think about what our next move should be, it may cost us points, and maybe even the match. We practiced these moves over and over again, so they would become more natural to us.

"The coaches emphasized the fact that wrestling is a sport where we must constantly review what has been taught in the past and then add more new moves during each practice. They spread all of us out over the mats in pairs to begin a review of several things. They made sure we had enough room so that we were not bumping into each other. The entire room is filled with mats on the floor, and the walls are padded so that no one can get injured if we were to hit the wall by accident. This gave everyone plenty of space to work.

"The first thing we reviewed was our stance. They made sure we were all doing the stance correctly. They emphasized that our stance was the same as the one a basketball player would use when guarding his opponent or a linebacker would use on the football field just before the ball was snapped."

John then stood up again and demonstrated the form that was needed. "Our coaches make sure our feet are spread out comfortably, with our bodies well balanced and above our feet. Our knees have to be slightly bent and our arms have to be bent at the elbows, with our elbows in against our sides. Our hands have to be slightly wider apart than our elbows and our hands are open. Our heads also have to be up so that we are looking at our opponent.

"The next thing we worked on was moving from side to side and forward and back.

We were told to never cross our feet. We have to step with our lead foot and then slide our trailing foot in the same direction as our lead foot. Every time we move, whether it is forward, backward, or to either side, we must step slide, step slide, step slide." John showed his parents the step slide technique and then sat back down at the table and continued eating his meal.

He went on telling them about practice. "The coaches moved throughout the room to make sure everyone was doing all of the moves correctly. They also explained that crossing our feet when moving gave our opponent an opportunity to attack our legs and possibly gain an advantage on us. It was very easy to trip someone if his feet are crossed, and it could result in our being taken down to the mat.

"In the next part of practice, they showed us how to do takedowns. Takedowns are where we try to take our opponents off of their feet and control them on the mat. First, we worked on some hand control techniques. They said it was very important to control our opponent's hands when trying to take him down to the mat.

"Coach Collona works with all of the light-weight wrestlers, but with me specifically, because I am just starting out. All of the coaches can help any of the wrestlers, but since I am so new, he concentrated on making sure I am doing everything as well as I can. We also spent quite a bit of time on the movement drill. We kept moving left, right, forward, and back. It is very important to be on balance as much as possible in any of the positions.

"We then worked on a single-leg takedown, and a double-leg takedown. They said we would be adding more takedown moves as practices continue. However, they want us to do these two takedowns before we move on to the others we will eventually need to know.

"The coaches explained to us that when using a single or double-leg takedown, we must use a penetrating step into our opponent. Then you attack his leg or legs. With the single-leg, you need to put both of your hands on one of his legs, then drive in and lift the leg at the same time. Your shoulder should give you enough leverage to take him to the mat.

"On the double-leg takedown, we have to step in low, but then lower our body even more, and bring his legs in as tight as we can, putting our head to one side or the other of his hips, and then lift him onto our shoulder. Then we tilt him away from our head, and use the head against his hip to help bring him to the mat. In both of these moves, we have to follow him to the mat and move our body up toward his head to maintain control.

"This was really all new to me because when I wrestled with Bill in his basement, we only did things on the floor. There was no room to try takedowns, and the floor was too hard for us to practice them anyway.

"During the next drill, we were put into a referee's position on the mat and practiced with another wrestler. They made sure that our hand and foot positions were correct. We were then shown several escape moves from the bottom position, including a stand-up move, a sit-out move, and a roll move.

"Then we were shown counter moves from the top position to each of the moves we made from the bottom. We spent quite a bit of time practicing these moves from both the bottom and top positions. They made sure we understood that we would always be reviewing before we moved on to new techniques.

"The next part of practice was spent showing us some pinning combinations. Most of the upper class boys knew these moves pretty well, but to most of the ninth and tenth graders, these were relatively new. Not all of the tenth graders had wrestled as ninth graders; so much of what I was learning was also new to them.

"We started with a relatively simple pinning combination called an arm bar with a half nelson. We do this when we have our opponent flat on the mat, face down. Usually, if we are right handed, we put in the arm bar with our left hand and arm between our opponent's left arm at the elbow, and then pull his arm toward us. Then we place our right arm under his right armpit and put our hand on the back of his neck with our palm toward the mat. By pulling his left arm toward us and pulling his head down with our right palm allows us to turn him onto his back. Then we move our chest onto his chest to make sure both of his shoulders or shoulder blades are touching the mat. Normally, we want to be perpendicular to him. This applies even more pressure to force his back onto the mat for the pin."

John stood up again and used his dad to demonstrate the arm bar with a half nelson on him. His dad said, "Don't hurt me!" and they all laughed.

"The coaches then showed us a reverse half nelson. We are taught to switch to this when we don't have enough pressure on our opponents chest. Not having enough pressure on his chest with the arm bar and half nelson allows our opponent to roll slightly away from us, which brings his inside shoulder up off the mat. In order to counter his move, we have to put our right arm under his neck and try to force his far shoulder to the mat by putting as much pressure on it with our hand. Then we have to move our chest forward to hold down his near shoulder."

Reverse half nelson

"They also tell us that in the half nelson, or reverse half nelson, we have to try to lift his buttocks in the air to put more pressure on his shoulders. We do this by lifting his buttocks with our other hand and arm.

"Then Coach Smith and his assistant coaches separated us into small groups by weight classes for the next drill. There are a total of thirty-two boys out for the wrestling team. Depending on the weights of the boys, there are usually four of us in each group. We then take our turn in the center of the group. Each of us in the group wrestles the boy in the middle. We do this one at a time, for two minutes each. We start on our feet with takedowns and then each of us wrestles the boy in the center. We try to get as many takedowns as we can in two minutes.

"After each wrestler has his turn in the middle doing takedowns, we start all over again in the referee's position. One of us will be on our hands and knees, and each of the others gets in the top position, one at a time. Our goal is to try to break down the bottom boy's stance. Pinning the boys in the middle is our ultimate goal if we can. This continues until all of us in each group have our turn in both the top and bottom positions.

"During these drills, the middle wrestler is not supposed to be like a tackling dummy. While we are trying to break him down, or pin him, he is also trying to escape from us or reverse us so that he is now on top. The only difference is that the person in the middle normally wrestles the longest time without a break. Then while the top wrestler goes into the middle, the rest of us can go for a drink, one at a time, to keep hydrated.

"While this portion of practice is going on, the coaches move from group to group to make sure that each of us is doing all of the moves correctly. This is not only a time to teach, but it's also a great conditioner. When these drills are over, all of us have wrestled well over the normal match time of six minutes. Each match is made up of three two-minute periods, unless it ends earlier because of a pin.

"Coach Smith explained to us, that while we are not in the middle, we can get water, juice, or Gatorade to drink. He told us that continually drinking fluids during practice is not just good for us, but is an excellent formula for making weight easier. He told us that we lose weight through our kidneys, and that is why drinking a lot of fluids helps stabilize our body weight.

"He told us that he had been to a wrestling clinic where famous college coaches came and spoke. One of the sessions dealt with making weight. The guest speaker told the audience that the best way to make sure wrestlers make weight for each match is to allow them to drink water, juice, or Gatorade whenever they are not actually wrestling during practice. This means that when we are not in the middle against other wrestlers, we are allowed to go over and get a quick drink.

"He said that he had much success with this formula for making weight at another school, where he had been an assistant wrestling coach. He explained to us that the reason he came to Claremont High School last season was because it was his first opportunity to become a head wrestling coach.

"Ready, Wrestle"

"He was always a firm believer in not having his team members cut weight. That is why he was really happy that the two tests Bill explained to you are now a standard rule for determining the lowest weight class for each wrestler on the team. I had to take the test the first day of practice, but I have nothing to worry about since I am in the lowest weight class, and I can actually afford to gain a few pounds."

When they were all finished eating, and the dishes were done, John went back upstairs to finish his homework and then got ready for bed. During the week, he did not watch much television. He preferred to read instead. When his homework was finished, he liked to read fiction just for enjoyment. He especially liked books by Jack London and other similar books. His parents expected him to be in bed by no later than 11:00 p.m., and it was sometimes earlier than that because he is wrestling now.

While John was upstairs, his parents were watching some TV and discussing how happy he seemed to be. His dad said,

"I think it was a great idea for John to have gotten into wrestling."

Then his mom added, "I think from the sound of things, the coaching staff really seems to care about their wrestlers as people, not just athletes they can train to perform." They were both very happy for John, and were excited to follow his progress as the season continued.

Chapter 5

The next day at practice, Coach Smith said to the boys, "Don't forget to remind your parents that this Thursday evening is parents' night. It starts at 7:00 p.m. and will last about an hour and a half. We sent them a flyer reminding them about this night. I want to make sure that as many of your parents can come to this as possible." He asked the boys to encourage their parents to attend.

Then he said, "The other coaches and I are extremely happy with the way all of you have been practicing. You all seem to be picking up everything that we have been throwing at you so far. I know that we are really moving fast to get you ready for the season. The opening match will be here before we know it."

When Thursday finally arrived, the coaches were pleased to see that all of the boys' parents had been able to come to this special night. Coach Smith said to the parents, "My main goal this evening is to introduce you to the sport which your sons have chosen. I feel you parents whose sons have never wrestled before might enjoy the matches more if you were more familiar with what is happening on the mat. I know that those of you whose sons have been wrestling for several years now are more familiar with the sport, the rules of the sport, and that many of you men may have wrestled in high school or college as well."

He added, "Since both of my assistant coaches are new to the school, I thought it was important to introduce them to all of you. They were both assistant coaches at the schools where they had previously taught and coached. Both of them also played football and wrestled in high school and college.

"Coach Benson teaches sophomore English and is going to be the new track coach, along with being one of my assistants. I have also made him the head JV wrestling coach as well. Coach Collona teaches physical education and health classes and is responsible for supervising the new weight room that was added to the gym building over the summer.

"I want you to understand as many wrestling maneuvers as we can show you this evening. You need to be aware of what is happening on the mat. The last thing we want is to have any of you yelling at the officials during a match. Anyone can make mistakes, and these officials do the best they can every time they step on the mat. Trust me; you will definitely know if I think that a wrong call was made." The coaches and the parents and wrestlers all laughed at this remark.

"My philosophy is that I trust my assistant coaches and all three of us help coach all of the boys. However, for practice purposes, I break up our responsibilities somewhat. Coach Collona is responsible for the first four weight classes (106, 113, 120, and 126). Coach Benson is responsible for the next five (132, 138, 145, 152, and 160), and I handle the last five weight classes (170, 182, 195, 220, and heavyweight).

"Ready, Wrestle"

"At all of our individual matches, the varsity and junior varsity teams will both be wrestling the opposing school's team at the same time on separate mats. There will be separate officials, timers, and scorekeepers for each mat. As mentioned earlier, Coach Benson will act as the JV head coach. Coach Collona will work with us wherever he is needed during the matches. He is very good at dealing with minor injuries, like cramps or bloody noses, and he will take care of that area for us."

Coach Smith said, "I'm sure that most of you know that the matches are made up of three periods, and each period is two minutes in length. Naturally, a pin or an injury would shorten the match. In the first period, the boys both start on their feet and the object is to take their opponent down to the mat for what is called a 'takedown.' Years ago, the referee would start the match by saying 'shake hands,' and then say, 'Ready, Wrestle'. Now the referee will indicate to the wrestlers to shake hands and give a hand signal as he blows his whistle."

Then the boys moved onto the mats and showed the parents several takedown moves, including a single-leg takedown, a double-leg takedown, and a fireman's carry takedown. He told the parents there are many other types of takedowns they might see, but these are the easiest to learn, so wrestlers will use them more often.

The next thing that was demonstrated was the referee's position. He had several boys show how the second and third periods started with this maneuver. He told them that the wrestlers would reverse positions in the third period if the match goes that long. He also said that some wrestlers might choose to start the second period in the neutral position, which was the same way the first period began.

Referee's Position

"This has been in effect for a few years now, but there is a new position some wrestlers prefer to use in the referee's position. The bottom boy's position remains the same as it has been for years. However, the top boy can now stand behind his opponent and place his hands on the small of the bottom wrestler's back. He makes a triangle by touching his thumb tips together, and then touching the first finger of each hand together to complete the triangle.

"The top boy may be better on his feet, so he can let his opponent escape without trying to stop him. His other option would be to attack his opponent from the standing position, but his leverage would be much better." He then had two of the boys demonstrate both maneuvers.

Next, he had the wrestlers show several types of pinning combinations, and told the parents that a pin was also called a fall. The wrestlers demonstrated both a fall and near-fall to show how they can accumulate back points.

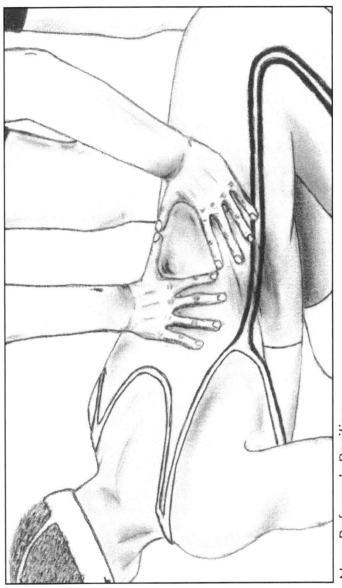

New Referee's Position

Coach Benson said, "Some of the boys are subject to nose bleeds during practice, and the same thing might happen in a regular match. In order to try to keep these nose bleeds to a minimum, you can help us limit the frequency of them by having your sons use a light coating of Vaseline in their noses at home from time to time."

He continued by explaining that bloody noses often happen because the blood vessels in the nose are close to the surface in the nose. "In the winter, these vessels can dry out and be subject to bleeding with even a light bump. Vaseline will help keep the blood vessels softer, and while your sons may still get an occasional bloody nose in a match, the frequency of them can be reduced."

He also added that there is another method for stopping nosebleeds. "This is to cauterize the vessels, which needs to be done in a doctor's office. A probe style tool burns the blood vessels. I know this sounds horrible, but it's not as bad as you might think. The reason this works is that the vessels grow thicker walls as they heal. This makes it more difficult for them to bleed."

Coach Collona said to the parents, "We have four wrestling managers who help us both during practice sessions and the regular matches. They are volunteers who are usually athletes in the fall season or spring seasons. They do not participate in winter sports but want to stay close to their friends. They have to wash the mats every day with a special disinfectant soap and hot water. Dirty mats can be the cause of many types of skin problems. We have to make sure we do not allow this to happen."

Coach Benson added, "There's always a medical kit in the wrestling room. This has various first aid items to use on small cuts, and ice packs for bruises. We use the ice packs to help prevent swelling. The managers always make sure the kit is available, and full of all of the items we might need at all times.

"The managers are also responsible for making sure there is plenty of liquid available at all times. We use water, juice, and

Gatorade, and the wrestlers can get a drink at any time if they are not involved on the mat during practice. We like to make sure they all stay hydrated."

He continued, "We even have smelling salts available in case someone accidentally hits his head too hard on the mat. If he feels a little groggy, we use the smelling salts to help clear his head. Also, all three of us are trained in first aid and can determine if the damage might be more serious. If that's the case, we make sure the boy gets to a doctor in a hurry.

"It's our school policy that there is a physician attending all of our home matches. He can assist us with injuries and make a decision as to whether or not a boy should be allowed to continue wrestling. Usually, the doctor we have at the matches has children who go to our school. If our doctor can't make it to an away match, then we check with the coaches from the school we are going to and ask if they have a doctor available."

Coach Smith took over again and said, "The next thing we want to cover involves additional ways our boys can score points against an opponent. The boys will demonstrate some of these for you. They include escaping from the bottom position; gaining control over their opponents by escaping or reversing positions; or, possibly by being awarded penalty points for an illegal hold or any other violation of the rules. Illegal holds are not generally done on purpose, but they might happen when the two wrestlers are scrambling for a controlling position.

"As those of you who have been around wrestling for some time know, the state makes weight allowances for each weight class to receive two extra pounds on Christmas Day. This is in effect to allow for the natural growth of the wrestlers as the season progresses. An additional pound is also added for the second day of a two-day tournament or the second day of a back to back dual meet when the second day is with a different team than the first day.

"I have four more things I want to briefly discuss before the night is over. The first is that there will be several practices and a tournament during the Christmas and New Year's vacations.

"The second thing is that there will be a scrimmage match with the team from Mt. Vernon Prep School on the Saturday after Thanksgiving. This will start at noon and the school will provide a bus for transportation. The parents will not be invited to attend because it will be held in Mt. Vernon Prep's wrestling room which cannot accommodate spectators.

"The third thing I want to mention is that there might be a good chance that one or more of your sons might end up wrestling a female wrestler somewhere down the road. There are many very good female wrestlers now wrestling in high schools in Ohio." Several of the parents were surprised by this announcement, and so were some of the boys.

"The last piece of information I want to pass along to you is a dual meet tournament. This is run slightly differently from a regular tournament because each team wrestles all of the other teams. Losing to a boy from one team does not eliminate someone from wrestling in the next team match. We currently do not have one of these on our schedule this season, but we probably will have at least one next year.

"If we have two boys in the same weight class who are very close in ability, I may want to let one boy compete against one team, and let the other boy wrestle against one of the other teams. This gives the second boy an opportunity to show that he can also wrestle well against good competition.

"We thank everyone for coming to the parents' night wrestling clinic and we hope to see you at all of the matches. It is always good to have our own cheering section, no matter where we are wrestling. If there are any questions you may have that we have not answered to your satisfaction, the other coaches and I will be happy to answer them while your sons are changing into their street clothes."

John and Bill's parents had come to the parents' night together in one car. Since they lived next door to each other, both boys naturally rode home with them. On the way home, both Bill and John said to their parents, "Neither one of us has any trouble making weight. May we stop at the local custard stand for ice cream?" Their parents said they thought that was a good idea. The adults all had cones and of course, the two boys ordered sundaes.

Chapter 6

John continued to keep his parents up to date as to his wrestling progress. He talked about it each night at the dinner table. "I'm very happy that the coaches are   pleased with the way I am developing as a wrestler. They keep telling me that they think I'm improving every day." John also said he was extremely happy with his coaches' praise. He said to his parents, "I'm just elated to be part of a varsity team at last."

School ended and Thanksgiving vacation had started. Coach Smith told the boys that the practices would start at 10:00 a.m. on Monday, Tuesday, and Wednesday, and that they would be finished by noon each day. He also said they would meet again on Saturday afternoon, two days after Thanksgiving. This would probably last only about an hour, and consist mainly of running.

"Ready, Wrestle"

The practices continued to go well for all of the wrestlers. The three days went by quickly and the team members were glad that Thanksgiving was the next day.. Both John and Bill's grandparents lived out of state and were too far away to come to their homes for Thanksgiving dinner. With the two boys having to practice during the break, and having a scrimmage match two days after the holiday, they would not have enough time to go visit their grandparents during the long weekend.

Earlier in the month, John's mom had asked Bill and his parents to share their holiday with them and they had accepted her invitation. Mrs. Thomas asked, "What can I bring to dinner?"

Mrs. Lester said, "It would be great if you would bring a vegetable dish and perhaps a pumpkin pie." Mrs. Thomas told her that she would bring both items.

They had all of the fixings that most people usually have at Thanksgiving dinner. There was turkey, mashed potatoes with brown gravy, sweet potatoes, vegetables, home-made bread and of course, pumpkin pie with whipped cream on top for dessert. Everyone ate their fill, and the boys' parents were becoming closer friends each time they got together to do things with the boys. Both of the boys were very happy to see this.

Chapter 7

There was a short practice on Friday afternoon at 2:00 p.m. the day after Thanksgiving. Coach Smith said, "This is just to loosen you up following your big Thanksgiving meal. We won't be here long, and we will not be practicing very hard today. We just want to work out a little so we are ready for tomorrow."

When the practice was over, the coaches had the boys sit on the mats so they could discuss tomorrow's scrimmage. Coach Smith said, "In many cases, when smaller schools compete against larger schools in sporting events, the larger schools come out ahead. The reason this happens is a matter of numbers. The larger schools have more male students from which to choose. It's not a foregone conclusion that they will always dominate the smaller school teams, but it happens more often than not. This scrimmage will not count on your individual wrestling records, and it will not affect the teams' record either. It's strictly a practice match against another team. We do not have them on our schedule during the regular season."

The Claremont coaches made their wrestlers aware that competing against people from a larger school would often help them wrestle better when they begin their matches against the smaller schools in their own division. They reminded them to be at the school tomorrow at noon to leave for the scrimmage against Mt. Vernon Prep School.

Chapter 8

When the school bus arrived at Mt. Vernon, the team got off the bus and went inside to change into their wrestling gear. John said to Bill, "I'm really excited about this. How do you think we'll do against them?"

Bill said, "I wrestled against them in last year's scrimmage and did really well. You should do fine, too."

When the team was all ready, they went out to the wrestling room and began to warm up. The Claremont coaches got together with the Mt. Vernon coaches and set up the schedule for the way the matches would be handled.

Coach Collona came up to John and told him that he would have two matches today. "The first one will be against a freshman and the second one will be against a sophomore wrestler." He said, "The tenth grader placed fifth in the big school state tournament last season. It will be a great experience for you to wrestle someone who is a very good wrestler."

John was excited, and a little nervous. His friend Bill said, "Wrestle each of them the way you have been working out during our practices and you'll do just fine." He also told John that Coach Collona had told him he was going to have two matches as well.

The Mt. Vernon coach had hired regular wrestling officials for the scrimmage. Most officials liked to get in some pre-season work to make sure they were also ready when the regular season started. This was always a good thing, because the boys got used to wrestling with regular officials, as opposed to having their coaches make the calls like they do in practice. This made it more realistic for everyone.

Coach Smith reminded the boys it's no longer necessary to wrestle from the lightest weight class to the heaviest weight class. He said, "The new rules have been changed in this way. The referee has fourteen cards marked one through fourteen. He pulls out one of the cards before the matches start, and whatever number he pulls will be the first match. For example, if he pulls out the number five, then the first match will be the 132-pound weight class. The other matches then follow in order up to Heavyweight and then down to the 106-pound class with the 126-pound class being the last match." He continued, "Since this is the first scrimmage of the year for both teams, we decided to just wrestle in regular order from the lightest to the heaviest."

The wrestling room at Mt. Vernon Prep was much larger than the one at Claremont. It was big enough to have four matches going on at one time. There was a pretty good chance that because of the size of the room, John and Bill might be wrestling at the same time. This meant that there was a possibility they would not be able to watch each other wrestle, at least not for their first match of the day.

Chapter 9

John was very nervous and it seemed as though his opponent was as well. The boys stood on their lines, red for the visitors and green for the home team, just like a regular match. The referee had a red wristband on one arm and a green one on the other arm. This would be the same for all of the matches they would wrestle including tournaments. The referee said, "Shake hands" and then blew his whistle for the start of the match.

Both boys began to circle each other and most of John's nervousness went away. They each tried a couple of different takedown moves, and both were able to counter the other's attempts.

John thought he had an opening when they were hand fighting for control. He immediately shot in on his opponent's legs and was able to use a double-leg takedown maneuver. It worked perfectly, just like in practice, and he brought his opponent to the mat. John received two points for the takedown. He then put his opponent in a bar arm half nelson pinning combination. He was hoping he could hold him there long enough and close enough to the mat to pin him, or earn back points.

His opponent was able to fight off of his back and John was awarded three more points for the near-fall. The match continued with them in the referee's position on the mat, with John on top. He rode his opponent for the remainder of the first period and did not score any more points.

John knew the scrimmage was being run like a tournament rather than a dual meet. Therefore, the referee flipped his red and green disk in the second period. It came up red and gave John a choice to make. John's coaches usually wanted their wrestlers to choose the top position, or the neutral position with both wrestlers on their feet. He felt very confident, having scored five points in the first period, and having come so close to pinning his opponent.

Therefore, he chose to remain in the neutral position with both of them on their feet. When the referee blew his whistle, John made his move and quickly took his opponent down, this time with a fireman's carry move. He rode his opponent for most of the second period and then just before time ran out, he put the other boy on his back and pinned him. He had made the right choice.

He was very happy. He shook hands with the boy he wrestled and his hand was raised to signify that he had won. Each of the boys said, "Nice match" to each other and left the mat.

John was able to watch Bill wrestle the remaining portion of his match because his had ended early with the pin. Bill defeated his opponent 8-1 and he was also very happy. Bill walked off the mat after his hand was raised and he and John shook hands and clapped each other on the back. They were both really happy.

Bill said, "There's plenty of room to still workout. Why don't you go over and roll around with the boy you wrestled, and I'll do the same thing with my opponent. It will keep us loose for our next match, and also show good sportsmanship."

John agreed that it would be a good thing to do, so he went over to his opponent and introduced himself. "My name is John Lester, what's yours?"

The other boy smiled, "My name is Brian McGregor, nice match." They talked for a few minutes and then they began to work out and practice various moves on each other.

John's second opponent was Mt. Vernon's first team 106-pound wrestler. He was the boy who had placed fifth in last season's state finals. He was a year older and a much better wrestler than the first boy John beat earlier. The match was a good one and John made the match very competitive. He lost by a score of 8-2, but everyone in the room was surprised by how well he wrestled.

The upper weight wrestlers were still going, so John and the two boys he wrestled got together and each ate an orange and drank some water to replenish their systems. They talked for a while and then took turns wrestling each other and trying different moves.

The older 106-pound wrestler worked with both John and the boy John wrestled in his first match. He talked to both of them about balance and body control. He told them, "These are two things you both should work on every day in practice." He added, "Not being strong in these two areas can get you into trouble, even when you are wrestling against boys who do not have the same level of skills as you have."

Bill won both of the matches he wrestled. He defeated his second opponent by a score of 6-2. He then did the same thing with the boys he wrestled that John had done with his opponents.

When the scrimmage was over, everyone shook hands and wished each other good luck for the coming season. The Claremont team took showers, got dressed, then got on the bus and headed back to school and then home.

Chapter 10

When John got home, he bombarded his parents with a blow-by-blow account of his matches. They were quite proud of John for having done so well in his first experience against boys from a larger school. They were very happy that he had also made friends with the boys he wrestled.

His dad commented, "Good sportsmanship is an important part of athletics and you have learned a very important lesson at your age. That is something you can carry with you for the rest of your life."

John replied, "Thanks Dad, our coaches always talk to us about being good sports."

John told his parents what was coming up next. "We have regular practices all of next week, and then next Friday, we will have our first conference meet at home at 7:30 p.m. We will have to be at the school by about 6:15 because we will start to weigh-in at 6:30 sharp. I will want to have my dinner at 4:30 so I won't be too full when we start to wrestle."

When John finished telling them about the weigh-ins, his mom said, "You must be pretty tired right now."

Yawning, he said, "I'm tired." His parents said they were also tired, so they all went up to bed. John did not read that night, but he was still pretty wound up about his matches. He lay in bed for quite some time thinking about everything that took place at the scrimmage that day.

Chapter 11

The next morning the family had breakfast together. Then John called Bill and suggested they go for a run. Bill said, "Okay." The weather was cold, but it felt good to John. He was still so excited from yesterday. He needed to run to burn off some of his excess energy.

When they were done running Bill said, "Going for a run was a great idea; it helped me to calm down."

John said, "Me too!"

Both of them said, "See you tomorrow," and went in the house.

When John came in from his run, his parents were in the family room reading the Sunday paper. His dad looked up from the paper and asked John how his run had gone. He said, "It was great."

"Ready, Wrestle"

His mom said, "Why don't you sit down and explain to us more about how the team is chosen."

John explained to his parents that most of the weight classes had more then one wrestler in them. "In order to determine who will wrestle varsity and who will wrestle JV, the coaches have challenge matches. These are also called wrestle-offs." He continued explaining the procedure to them. "These matches normally take place on Wednesday. This gives us a practice day before the next match. Each winner of the challenge match will be varsity, and the one who loses will wrestle JV. If there are three boys in a weight class, they have to have at least two matches to determine who the varsity and JV wrestlers will be."

John said, "Since I'm the only 106-pound wrestler on the team, I'm automatically the varsity wrestler." He also explained that the JV team has to forfeit the 106-pound weight class, and the team score will be 6-0 in favor of their opponents before the match even starts. These are the same number of points a team would receive for a pin."

John continued, explaining other situations to his folks. "When there are three or more wrestlers in a weight class, the coaches in the league try to match up the extra wrestlers against their extra boys, so that all of the boys on the team will have an opportunity to wrestle. There are times when a boy wrestling one of the extra matches may have to wrestle someone who is a weight class above or below his weight in order for him to have a match."

John continued, "The extra matches are usually wrestled on the junior varsity mat when the regulars are done wrestling. The scores of the extra boys' matches do not count for either the varsity or JV teams, but the boys are happy to get the experience of wrestling in front of a big crowd." He said, "Another reason everyone gets to wrestle is that the coaches never know when one of the JV wrestlers may have to fill in for a varsity wrestler who gets injured. This also means one of the extra boys will move into the JV line-up to fill that weight class."

His mom said, "That was a good explana-
tion, and I feel I'm beginning to understand
more and more about the sport."

Chapter 12

On Monday, after the Thanksgiving break, Coach Smith said to the boys, "Coach Benson, Coach Collona, and I are very pleased with the quality of wrestling we saw at the scrimmage. It shows how hard you have all been working to get better. We need to continue working hard at every practice so that we continue to improve each week."

As usual, the coaches continued to put emphasis on all of the wrestlers doing their homework each night. "We want you to make sure you stay eligible to wrestle. Also, it's important for your future to continue learning as much as possible while you are in high school," Coach Benson said to them.

Coach Collona added, "Not all high school graduates continue on to college, but a good educational foundation is important. Regardless of the kind of job you may have later in life, you must always know how to read, write, and use some basic math skills."

The wrestling practices continued to try to advance the skills of all of the boys. There was always repetition of the previous moves they were taught, and new moves were added on a regular basis. Some members of the team were further advanced than others and were shown technical moves that not everyone could master at this time.

Bill and some of the more experienced wrestlers were being taught a cross-body ride and a figure four ride. Both of these had pinning combinations which could be used against their opponents and would help them as the competition became tougher during the season. These two maneuvers were excellent for controlling an opponent when he was on his hands and knees.

Coach Collona explained that these moves were best used by boys who were rather tall and had long muscles instead of short, more bulky muscles. He said, "Bill Thomas and the Sommers brothers have perfect bodies for these moves. Bill is rather tall for his age, with fairly long arms and legs and he is strong. The Sommers twins are six foot two inches tall and they are also strong." John Lester was also included in the group to learn some of these leg rides because he had fairly long arms and legs too.

In addition to these varsity wrestlers, there were some JV wrestlers who might develop into pretty good leg wrestlers. They were Mike Sommers, the twins' freshman younger brother, who wrestled at 113. Because he was tall for his age, the coaches wanted him to work on these moves too. There was also Bob Browning, another freshman, who wrestled JV at 160 pounds. They all had similar body types with fairly long arms and legs.

Coach Collona said, "When using the cross-body ride, you have to use your left leg and put it between the bottom wrestler's legs from front to back and hook his left ankle with your ankle. Then move your body across your opponent's lower back, rather than parallel to him. Your left hipbone should be high up on his back as well. Use your right arm to control his right leg by grabbing the ankle. Control his head with your left arm by applying pressure to the side of his head. You then rotate your hip down while lifting his right knee to the outside. This should break him down flat on the mat. This will open up a series of pinning combinations including a half nelson and possibly a cradle.

"The other move I want you to learn is the figure four. In this move, you put your left leg under your opponent's hip area and straight across his body. Then hook your left foot behind your own right leg at the knee. While doing this, you can grab his left arm with your left arm and use it like an arm bar. Then you can reach up and put in a half nelson with your right arm. You need to learn to use these moves from either the right or left side of your opponent."

Coach Collona worked with his group by practicing these two leg rides so that they could add both of them to the other types of controlling rides and pinning combinations the team had been working on all along.

Coach Smith also reminded all of the boys that it's important to continue to use a series of moves. "This is necessary so that if your opponent counters your initial move, you can follow up with another in the series to counter his counter move. The moves have to become second nature to you. It should not be something you have to think about, you just need to flow into the next move naturally."

The first real matches of the year were getting nearer now. It was still fun to work out in the wrestling room, but the boys could feel that the coaches were allowing much less joking around during practice. All of the wrestlers seemed to be improving and the practices were definitely more intense.

Chapter 13

The first dual meet of the year was coming up on the next Friday night. All of the challenge matches had taken place, and the varsity and junior varsity teams were established. Some of the wrestlers might change from match to match, depending on the outcome of the challenge matches, but for the most part, the varsity wrestlers would be the same for most matches, barring injuries.

John and Bill knew they were more than likely to be permanent in their weight classes, unless one of them was injured. In John's case, if he got injured, the team would have to forfeit his weight class, since he was the only 106-pound wrestler on the squad.

Because their sons were best friends, their parents had gotten to be much closer friends too. In the past, they had done a few neighborhood things together, but now they began to socialize even more. When the coaching staff had held the parents' night practice to introduce the new parents to wrestling, they had also met many of the other wrestlers' parents as well.

However, they did not really know what a tight-knit group the wrestling parents were. They found out that after most of the home matches, one of the families would host an after-match get together, and all of the parents and boys were invited. They usually took turns hosting the parties. All of the parents would sit together at the matches and cheer for each other's boys during the match. Mr. and Mrs. Lester thought this was pretty unique, because nothing like this took place after the football games. They decided to volunteer to host the after-party following the next home match. Mr. and Mrs. Kelly, Lucas Kelly's mom and dad, had already chosen to host the one after the Hilliard High School match.

Chapter 14

Hilliard High School was one of the other nine schools in Claremont High School's League. All of the schools in the league were Division III schools. Hilliard would be the first home match of the season. They would also have some additional matches against several schools which were not in their league, but were normally on the schedule each year. These were called independent matches, but they counted on both the schools' and individual wrestlers' records. There would be five independent matches to fill out the schedule.

When Friday finally arrived, both teams weighed in as per the new rules which stated that both wrestlers in each weight class must weigh in at the same time. This also included both JV teams as well. All of the boys from both teams completed weighing in and everyone made weight. The referee made the draw to see which weight class would start the wrestling. He pulled out the number 8 which meant the first match wrestled would be at 145 pounds.

The Claremont coaches all thought that would be good for John. He would not have to be the first wrestler on the mat in his first varsity match. This would give him a chance to adjust to the excitement of his first match before he had to wrestle.

Senior Frankie Scaletti would be the first wrestler for Claremont. He's a very good wrestler and was able to get the first takedown early in the match. His opponent was also a senior and he was able to escape from Frankie after about a minute into the first period. They both made several attempts to win a takedown, but spent the rest of the period on their feet.

Claremont won the original coin toss to see which team would have the choice of positions in the second period. They had chosen the even matches. Frankie's opponent chose the bottom position to start the second period because he had escaped from Frankie earlier. This time, Frankie was able to counter his opponent's escape attempts and then broke him down flat on the mat. He used an arm bar with a half nelson and put his opponent on his back and pinned him with about thirty seconds left in the second period.

The remaining upper weights, from Freddie Sommers at 152 pounds and up, did very well. Freddie Sommers, John Thompson at 170 pounds, Lucas Kelly at 182 pounds, Marty Zone at 195 pounds, and Jim Hauser at 220 all won by decisions. David Sommers and Jim Flaherty both won with pins.

John's teammates were doing very well, and when it was his turn to wrestle, he was anxious but ready. John was wrestling a tenth grader, but he was ready to go when the referee blew his whistle to start the match. John circled his opponent moving to his left and then coming back quickly to the right and driving in for a single-leg takedown. He received his two points for the takedown when he established control on the mat.

John maintained control of his opponent for more than a minute. However, the other boy worked his way up to a standing position and escaped from John. He received one point for the escape move and they remained on their feet for the rest of the first period.

It was the Hilliard boy's choice of positions in the second period, and he chose the top position on the mat. The referee blew his whistle to start them, and the Hilliard boy put in a tight waist ride and controlled John for a full minute. No matter what he tried, John could not escape from, or reverse his opponent. They were both wrestling furiously and ended up going out of bounds.

They returned to the center of the mat and John was still in the bottom position. The referee blew his whistle to start them, and John tried a standing switch and reversed his opponent. This gave him two points for the reversal.

He now had a 4-1 lead in the match. They continued to struggle against each other, but John finally broke down his opponent's base, and was able to put him in a half nelson pinning combination. This earned him a three point near-fall as time ran out on the third period.

John was ecstatic about winning his first varsity match 7-1, but in a show of good sportsmanship, he did not jump around or do anything else that might embarrass his opponent. The boys shook hands and the referee raised John's hand to signal that he had won his first varsity match.

The next four matches were also victories for Claremont, including his best friend Bill who pinned his opponent in the third period. Junior Jim Budd at 120 pounds, senior Billie Mayfield at 126 pounds, and Donnie Jones at 132 pounds all won their matches. Bob Packard was the 138-pound wrestler who was up next. Bob was only a freshman and was going up against a very good junior from Hilliard. He was pinned in the second period. Since they had started wrestling with the 145-pound match, the 138-pound match was the last of the evening. The Claremont team won the match 48-9.

Chapter 15

Mid-term grades came out shortly after the first match of the season. Two of the ninth grade boys on the team had low grades in their math classes. They were Bob Packard at 138 pounds on the varsity, and Bob Browning at 160 pounds on the JV. John was an "A" student in math and volunteered to help them. They arranged a time that was convenient for the three of them and they met in a study hall three times a week.

All athletes at Claremont had to have eligibility sheets signed each week by their teachers in order to continue to participate in sports. Because John was helping the two boys in math, the math teacher was willing to continue to sign the two boys' eligibility sheets, as long as the tutoring continued. Both boys' test scores began to improve immediately and the math teacher continued to sign the sheets. The coaching staff was very happy that with John's help, both boys were able to continue to wrestle.

The first independent match after the Thanksgiving break was against a Division II school named Fairfield High. Most matches were scheduled for either a Tuesday afternoon, or a Friday evening. There were weeks when they had to wrestle twice in one week. The Fairfield match was scheduled for a Tuesday afternoon at Fairfield.

John wrestled a very good match, but lost to the boy from Fairfield High. His match was very close and could have gone either way, but he lost 5-4. He was a little unhappy, but Fairfield was a Division II school and his coaches were very happy with the way he had wrestled.

Bill won his match against his opponent with a pin, and five other teammates also won their matches. The other wrestlers who won were all seniors. They were Billie Mayfield at 126, Frankie Scaletti at 145, Lucas Kelly at 182, Marty Zone at 195, and Jim Flaherty at Heavyweight. However, it was not enough to win the overall match and Claremont lost by a score of 33-27.

The Jr. Varsity team had won their first match against Hilliard and had also lost their second match to the Fairfield JV team. The coaches were happy with the junior varsity showing so far. Each team had a record of 1-1. John's parents were very happy with the way he had handled his loss to his opponent. They loved seeing how happy he was to be wrestling varsity and that he was able to put his loss behind him and get ready for whatever came next. His mom said, "We have already volunteered to host the after-match party following the next Friday evening match against Uniontown Local."

John said to his parents, "There's going to be a JV Tournament coming up on Saturday at Riverton High School. This will be an eight-team tournament, and Coach Benson called the athletic director at Riverton High School to see if they would let me wrestle at 106 pounds. He explained to the A.D. that I am the varsity 106-pound wrestler, but I'm only a freshman, and I'm the only

106-pound wrestler we have. He also mentioned that I will only have wrestled two varsity matches."

He continued, "The athletic director said it would be fine to bring me to wrestle. It looks like all of the other teams will have full rosters for this tournament."

The entire junior varsity team arrived at 11:00 a.m. for weigh-ins. This included all of the boys who had lost in the wrestle-offs. Coach Benson had everyone weigh in just in case someone from one of the other schools did not make weight. If any of the extra Claremont boys got to wrestle, they would wrestle as an independent, and their scores would not count for the Claremont team score.

This would prevent having any openings in any weight class, and it would give some of the extra boys an opportunity to wrestle in a tournament. It would be a great experience for the boys if it happened. However, all of the wrestlers from the other teams made weight.

Chapter 16

The head referee for the tournament pulled a number before the first match and pulled out the number one. This meant that the wrestling would be done in the normal order of the weight classes. John would be the first one to wrestle and the heavyweights would be last.

The tournament started promptly at 1:00 p.m. and John was wrestling on mat one. According to Coach Benson, his opponent was a sophomore who had not wrestled as a freshman. When the referee blew his whistle to start the match, John wasted no time. He immediately attacked his opponent and used a double-leg takedown maneuver. John took the boy to the mat and rode him the whole first period. His opponent was very strong, and John never put him on his back.

After briefly discussing his strategy with Coach Benson during the short break between the first and second period, John chose the down position in the second period. On the whistle, John tried a stand-up move and was able to escape right away. His theory had proven to be correct. He had told Coach Benson, "I feel that, while my opponent is very strong, he may not know enough wrestling to keep me from escaping." His theory had worked to perfection.

John went on the attack again, and this time he used a single-leg takedown move and received two more points for another takedown. He was now leading 5-1 and was able to keep his opponent from escaping. In the third period, John was in the top position and rode out the other boy for most of the period. He could tell his opponent was getting tired and he rode him long enough to get a point for riding time. He won the match 6-1.

Since none of the extra Claremont wrestlers who weighed in had gotten to wrestle in the tournament, they remained there to watch and cheer for their teammates. The

Claremont team had done pretty well in the first round and they led the team scoring up to that point.

One sophomore and five of the juniors had made it through the first round, in addition to John. Two of them won by decisions and four had pins. This gave the team a total of eleven points going into the next session, which was scheduled to start again at 3:00 p.m.

John wrestled another sophomore in the second round. This boy was not as strong as the boy he wrestled earlier, but he was a much better wrestler. It was a whirlwind type of match with each of them taking each other down, escaping from the other, and then doing it again. The score was 5-5 after the first period.

In the second period, John had the advantage by having ridden out his opponent for most of the period. He built up enough riding time to earn a point. The boy he was wrestling rode John for most of the third period which canceled out John's riding time point. But with less than a minute left,

"Ready, Wrestle"

John was able to reverse his opponent and ride him until time ran out to win 7-5. He had made it to the finals and would be wrestling for the championship later that evening.

The other boys who got through the second round were sophomore Jamie Zone, and juniors Marty Chester, Tony Simpson, and the three upper weight boys, Larry Dolan, Chris Michaels, and Chester Grant. The three upper weight boys were also juniors.

Coach Benson said, "Many eight-team tournaments are set up as single elimination tournaments. This one will be a double elimination tournament and means there will be a consolation bracket to determine the third and fourth place winners. The losing wrestler in each weight class in the first round will have a second opportunity to wrestle against the other wrestler in the same weight class who also lost in the first round. This gives one of them a chance to try to come back and get into third or fourth place. Each of the two boys who lost in the first round, but won in the wrestle backs, must wrestle two more matches and win both of them in order to finish in third place."

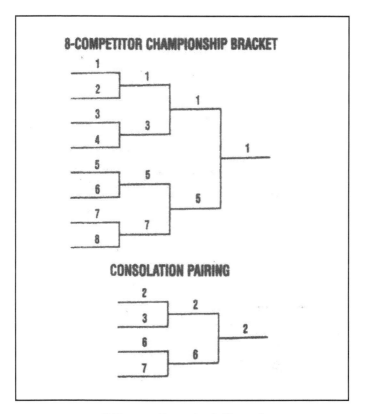

8 Team Bracket Sheet

Jamie Zone won his second match with a pin and was in the finals that evening. Tony Simpson and Larry Dolan each got into the finals by winning on points. Chris Michaels and Chester Grant won with pins and were also in the finals. This gave Claremont a total of twenty points and a good lead over the second place team which had fourteen points and only four boys in the finals.

Of the remaining eight Claremont wrestlers, three of them had come through wrestle backs by winning two matches and were going to be wrestling for third or fourth place in the evening matches. This gave their team an additional six points entering the finals. They now had a total of twenty-six points and an insurmountable lead. No team would be able to catch them no matter what happened in the final round.

The finals were not scheduled to start until 7:30 p.m. so most of the teams went out to eat. Some of the other teams had brought food with them and chose to stay and rest on the mats after they ate.

Coach Smith had been watching his JV team perform and he was very happy with what he had been seeing so far. When the Claremont team, and Coach Benson and Coach Collona went out to dinner, Coach Smith joined them. They all got on the team bus and drove to a nice local restaurant called Mom's. They had a good meal, but did not eat too much food. The last thing they wanted to do was to overeat and then not be able to wrestle to their abilities in the finals.

They arrived back at Riverton High School with plenty of time to get dressed in their uniforms and warm up again. They had each been given a second uniform so they had a dry one for the finals. These were old uniforms from last season that were in good enough shape to still be used for something like this. The boys were introduced by weight class just like they would be at the Sectional, District, and State tournaments.

Chapter 17

The referees, having followed the new rules for both dual meets and tournaments, made sure that wrestling the first match of the second round had been the 113-pound weight class. This meant that John would wrestle the last match in that round. Now, in the finals, the first match would be the 120-pound weight class, and John would wrestle second to the last one.

John seemed pretty nervous since this was his first tournament of any kind. He had never done anything like this before in front of such a large crowd. There were more people there than there had been at any of the earlier matches that day. The seats in the bleachers were completely filled, and there were also many people standing.

John's mom and dad had ridden to the matches with Bill's parents and this would be the first time John's parents had ever been to a tournament. The tension was more noticeable than the regular matches they had watched.

John's dad had run cross country and track in high school and college, and his mom had gone to an all girls Catholic school and participated in field hockey. Even so, they were both still extremely nervous getting ready to watch John in the finals.

The boy John was wrestling was from the host school of Riverton. He was a sophomore and had wrestled well in his previous two matches to get to the finals against John. When the referee blew his whistle, the Riverton boy immediately took John down with a fireman's carry move. John was shocked because he had never been taken down so early in a match before.

He really worked hard to get to a stand-up move and very quickly did a standing switch, which is a powerful move and often hard to stop. He reversed the other boy and the score was tied 2-2. They remained that way until late in the first period when the

Riverton boy was able to escape. Time ran out on them and John was losing 3-2.

John won the toss and chose to take the top position to start the second period. This was always the strategy of his coaches, since they worked so hard on controlling opponents in the second and third periods. John immediately threw in the legs, with a cross-body ride. This seemed to confuse his opponent, and John rode him hard. He was able to turn the boy to his back twice without losing his leg ride. He scored points each time. He could tell the cross body was wearing down his opponent, and John pinned him before time ran out in the second period. John won his first ever tournament.

His coaches were practically speechless because wrestling was so new to him. Coach Benson looked at Coach Collona and said, "Can you believe this kid? He's only been working on leg rides for two weeks now and he uses it in the finals to finish first."

Coach Collona just shook his head and responded, "This youngster may just be the real deal."

"Ready, Wrestle"

John's best friend Bill and the rest of the varsity team were at the finals. Naturally, Coach Smith had been there all day to watch the JV team wrestle in their first tournament. He was extremely happy with the way they all had wrestled.

All of the other boys won their final matches and they had outscored the other teams by so much, the championship was decided before the 220-pound and heavyweight matches were even wrestled.

John finished second to his teammate Chester Grant, the Heavyweight Champion, in the voting for the MVP award. Chester won it because his weight class was a really tough one, and he had pinned all of his opponents.

The Riverton Athletic Director came over to Coach Smith and the other Claremont coaches and said, "You have a fine young wrestler in John Lester. It's hard to believe he's just starting his first season. He really looks like a seasoned veteran. I wish you and your team good luck for the season. Congratulations for your fine victory."

John's coaches were quite happy as well. They were pretty sure they had struck gold with John and were looking forward to the season with him at 106 pounds. They were also pleased with the other boys as well. It showed that if someone on the varsity were to get injured, they would have some very capable replacements on the JV team.

On the way home from the tournament in the car his mom and dad, his best friend Bill, and Bill's parents, were all having a great time replaying what had taken place. Bill told John, "The matches you won today will not be counted on your record when seeding time comes for the Sectional Tournament. No JV matches can count for a varsity wrestler's record."

John said, "That makes sense, but I was not sure how that worked. I'm glad you explained it to me."

Chapter 18

The Christmas and New Year's vacation was approaching rather quickly. Wrestling practices would continue into the holiday vacation, as the team was entered in a holiday wrestling tournament which included teams from all three divisions. This would be held shortly after Christmas on December 29th and 30th. It was a sixteen-team tournament to be held at Cortland West High School.

There would be no separation by division in this tournament. All of the boys would be wrestling against opponents from other divisions, as well as their own division. This would be a huge test for the Claremont team since they were in Division III, the small school division.

"Ready, Wrestle"

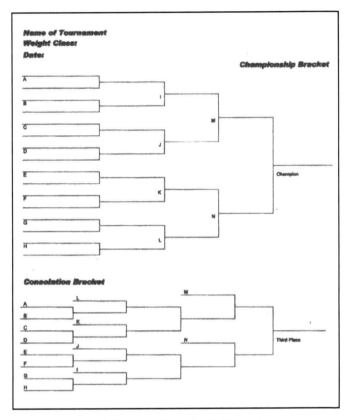

16 Team Bracket Sheet

The whole team was a little nervous about wrestling in this tournament because they might be wrestling several matches against Division I wrestlers. They were well aware that the larger schools had more athletes from which to choose for all of their sports.

Their coaches assured them that whether they won or lost, the experience would help them tremendously when they got back to wrestling in their own conference.

At the seeding meeting for this tournament, the Claremont coaches did not have much luck placing their wrestlers. In fact, the only boys who were seeded in the top four slots in their weight classes were the seniors. They had good records from the previous season and this helped them all get into the top four spots in their weight classes.

Billie Mayfield and Marty Zone both got seeded fourth. Frankie Scaletti was seeded in the third spot, and Lucas Kelly was seeded second. The only number one seed Claremont had was Jim Flaherty at Heavyweight. He was the Division III defending state champion and none of the other heavyweights had placed higher then third in their divisions the previous year.

John wrestled extremely well and won his first match against a sophomore from another team in Claremont's division. However, in his next match, he lost to a Division I wrestler and had to go through the consolation bracket in order to try to stay in the tournament and possibly finish in fifth or sixth place.

He came through the consolation bracket to finish fifth in the tournament. His final opponent was the boy from Central High, who had defeated him earlier in the year. John was able to show a lot of improvement since the first weeks of practice had begun. He defeated the Central High boy 6-3. He was elated to have placed and did it by avenging his first loss.

Bill continued his winning ways and wrestled four great matches to remain unbeaten for the season. He did not pin all of his opponents because he wrestled two boys from Division I and they were both very good wrestlers. He did pin the boy in his third match, and then won in the finals by a score of 7-3. The boy he beat in the finals was from Division II, and he had placed fifth in the state last season.

Billie Mayfield and Marty Zone both finished in fourth place, each having wrestled boys from Division I. Frankie Scaletti finished third, and Lucas Kelly finished second. Jim Flaherty won the heavyweight championship proving his Division III state championship the previous year was no fluke.

Coach Smith said to the team, "Coach Benson, Coach Collona, and I are extremely happy with the way all of you wrestled in this big school tournament. It shows that we are very solid as a team. Placing sixth in this tournament is a terrific accomplishment, considering the quality of overall wrestling we faced here. There will not be any more practices until school starts again on the fifth of January. We suggest that all of you do some running over the holiday vacation." He continued by saying, "Be careful about what you eat during your time off. Maintaining your weight over the break in the schedule will help you a lot when you come back."

Chapter 19

Many of the boys' families belonged to the YMCA and they could run indoors on the track there. However, the weather had been mild, and there was not much snow on the ground. So if they were careful, they could run outside as well. They knew the running would help them to maintain the degree of conditioning they had achieved so far. They also realized that working out would help them make weight easier when they came back to school.

John and Bill, and many of the other wrestlers, took the coaches' advice and went to the "Y" every day. They even rolled around a little on the mats that people used for an exercise class the "Y" had for adults in the evening.

When they returned to school after the first of the year, they began to have regular practices again. No one had gained too much weight, so the varsity team remained the same for their first match back. This was proof positive that the boys had all listened to their coaches and working out had been a good idea.

The next match of the season was within their conference on a Tuesday afternoon at Belleville High School. The boys were wrestling well, and John and Bill had both won their matches. John won on a decision, 8-4, and Bill pinned his opponent in the second period. It was always a good way to start the matches. Winning the first two matches really got everyone else pumped up. Claremont won the match by a score of 48-15. The JV team won its match as well.

There was one sour note during the match though. In the 132-pound weight class, Donnie Jones had been taken down by his opponent near the edge of the mat and they went out of bounds. Donnie hit his elbow on the gym floor. An injury time-out was called by the referee, and it was decided   after the two-minute injury time had run out, that he would not be able to continue wrestling.

The Belleville team was awarded six points, the same score as if Donnie had been pinned. This turned out to be a blow to the team because Donnie was a very good wrestler. However, it would be an opportunity for Bill Scaletti, Frankie's brother, the JV boy in that weight class to wrestle some varsity matches as his replacement. Claremont won the team match, but everyone was sad to have lost Donnie for at least a couple of weeks.

Marty Chester and Alan Lentine were two juniors in Donnie's weight class, and Harry Striker was a sophomore in the 132-pound weight class as well. Alan Lentine defeated Harry in the first wrestle-off, and then Marty defeated Alan in the second one the next day at practice. This made Marty the Varsity wrestler and Alan became the JV wrestler in the 132-pound weight class.

Their next match was at home against another conference rival, Uniontown Local High School on the following Friday evening. Uniontown would be a tough match as they had been the conference champions the previous season. However, they had graduated many of their best wrestlers. This might not make much difference in the match though, since their JV team had also been very strong.

As usual, to start the match the referee pulled a card out and the first match would be the 170-pound weight class. The Claremont coaches were quite happy with this draw because their upper weights were really strong. The upper weight boys continued their winning ways, but in the 182-pound match, Lucas Kelly was hit in the nose by an accidental elbow from his opponent and it began to bleed. There was an official time-out to stop the nosebleed.

Coach Collona went to the edge of the mat with a towel to help stop the bleeding. He held a towel to Lucas's nose and put pressure on his nose as well. He said to Lucas, "Have you been using Vaseline?"

Lucas responded, "Yes I have, but I have a slight cold and have been blowing my nose quite a lot and it has been sore." The nosebleed turned out to be just a minor injury, and Lucas went on to pin his opponent.

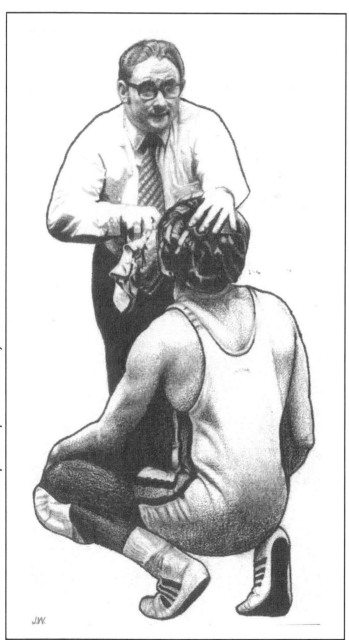

Coach Collona helps stop a bloody nose

In the middle of the line up, Uniontown was able to close the gap somewhat and the score was closer than Coach Smith, and his assistants were hoping it would be. Coach Smith said to his two coaches, "I expected there might be a couple of surprises waiting for us in this match, but this is too close for comfort to suit me." Both of his assistants agreed with him.

A couple of their best wrestlers, Marty Zone and Billie Mayfield, were held to tie matches. This gave each team two team points. There is no overtime wrestling in dual meets.

John Lester won a very tough match by a score of 8-6 at 106 pounds and Bill Thomas continued his winning ways by pinning his opponent. These two matches were very helpful in keeping the team undefeated in the conference. The final score against Uniontown was 37-22.

John's parents had earlier told all of the wrestlers' parents that they would host the party after the next home match. They invited everyone back to their home and served Sloppy Joes, homemade French fries, pasta salad and ice cream and a cheese cake for dessert. All of the parents made sure their sons did not eat too much dessert. The last thing they wanted was for someone to miss making weight the next match. Everyone thanked the Lesters and left feeling full and happy.

Chapter 20

The team continued its winning ways in their conference. They defeated all of the teams, and some of the boys remained undefeated. The team defeated Middleton, Allentown East, Saint Johns, Ridgewood, Mountainside, and Morton Center.

In addition to the conference matches, they also wrestled five independent matches against non-conference schools to finish off their season. These included Division II schools, Fairfield, Lincoln, and Riverside. Their other two wins were against Division III schools. These were Parkview and Eastside.

Marty Chester had a chance to wrestle four varsity matches as a substitute for Donnie Jones at 132 pounds, and his varsity record was three wins and one loss. Donnie came back after his elbow healed and continued his winning ways. His overall record was eight wins and two losses.

"Ready, Wrestle"

Claremont, having gone undefeated in the conference, was awarded the conference championship. Several of the boys also went undefeated in the conference and felt ready to move on to the sectionals.

The undefeated boys were Bill Thomas, Billie Mayfield, Marty Zone, although Billie and Marty each had one tie on their records. Lucas Kelly, Jim Hauser, and Jim Flaherty were also undefeated. John Lester, Frankie Scaletti, Freddie and David Sommers all finished at ten and four and John Thompson finished with a record of nine and five. The matches from the big school tournament would also be added to their records for seeding purposes.

Chapter 21

The sectional tournaments were coming up for all three divisions. These would be held in separate locations for each of the divisions in the state. Division I included all of the largest schools. This was measured by the number of male students attending each school. There were three locations in the state for the Division I schools, one in the north, one in the central area, and the other in the southern area.

Division II had two separate locations. One of these was located in the north central area of the state and the other one was located in the south central area. This was done in order to limit travel for all of the participating schools.

Division III was also held in two separate locations. Again, these were also held in the north and south central regions of the state to limit travel. For each of the divisions in the state, the top six place winners of the three divisions would move on to the next tournament, called the district tournament.

Prior to the start of the sectionals, the three coaches were gathered in the athletic office discussing their prospects for next season. During the regular season just finished, they had been going to the Ohio Youth Wrestling Association (OYWA) matches on weekends to watch younger wrestlers perform. These were elementary and junior high school age wrestlers.

Coach Smith said to his coaches, "When John Lester came out for the team, we all felt that he and Bill Thomas might be able to wrestle at the 106 and 113-pound weight classes again next year. Seeing them both now, having grown taller and gaining weight as well, we should probably reconsider our original thoughts." Both coaches agreed.

Coach Benson said, "John had been weighing in at about 100 pounds for much of the season, and now he is weighing in at 105 pounds. He is not having any trouble making weight but he has grown more than an inch taller then when the season started, and his additional weight is all muscle because of the weight lifting work-outs."

Coach Collona then said, "After meeting John's parents, I feel he is going to continue to grow in height. When we met his parents, the dad was about six foot three and his mother looked to be about five ten, pretty tall for a woman. John will probably grow enough to wrestle at 113 pounds next season."

They all agreed that Bill Thomas is in the same boat. He is now weighing in at the maximum weight for his class, which was up to 115 pounds with the Christmas weight allowance. He has also been really working hard in the weight room along with John and the rest of the team.

They decided that they would continue to go to the OYWA matches on weekends to watch some of the younger and lighter wrestlers perform. These boys would be likely candidates to replace John and Bill in the two lower weight classes. Then they would look at some of the wrestlers in any weight class who might not be going to Catholic high schools, or other private schools.

Coach Smith said, "We can't really do much in the way of actually recruiting these youngsters, but our just being there shows our interest in having some of these wrestlers attend Claremont."

Coach Benson added, "Catholic schools charge tuition and not every family can afford to send their children to private schools. Since many of the CYO and YMCA programs have joined the OYWA, our best chance to get some of these young wrestlers to attend Claremont means we have to pay more attention to the OYWA tournaments."

Coach Collona said, "There's a slim chance to have a small number of wrestlers who may not be able to afford a Catholic Jr. High school because of the finances. They may come to Claremont instead." He then added, "I've seen a couple of the light weight wrestlers who, if they came to Claremont next season, might be ready to wrestle varsity and junior varsity at 106 pounds, especially if they are aware that John would be moving up in class, at least to 113. It sure would be nice if we could fill in all of the lower weight classes next year on both the varsity and JV teams."

They knew that they might also have a chance to get some of the upper weight wrestlers to come to Claremont as well. They decided to pursue this project and would continue to attend the matches on weekends until the OYWA season ends. They also knew that if they happened to win the Division III State Championship, this would increase their chances of getting some of these young wrestlers to come to Claremont just to be in their program.

Chapter 22

They were now very busy getting their team ready to enter the sectional tournament. Practices were tough on the boys, but were shorter in duration so they did not have a group of tired wrestlers going into the long grind of three major tournaments in three weeks. When the sectional tournament weekend finally arrived, everyone felt as though they were really ready to wrestle their best.

In all of the next three weekends of wrestling, each bracket would be set up for sixteen wrestlers. The wrestlers in each weight class had to win their first four matches in order to be a champion. Any wrestler who lost to the boys who make it to the championship match had to wrestle two or three additional matches to finish in third place. This depended in which round they lost to the eventual champion.

"Ready, Wrestle"

Bill Thomas had the match of the tournament in the first round when it turned out that his opponent was a female wrestler from a small school in the southern part of Ohio. She was from Huntersville, Ohio, and was a pretty good wrestler to have gotten into the sectional tournament.

His teammates were really giving him the business and saying he better not lose to a girl. She was a good wrestler, but Bill was definitely the best wrestler in his weight class. However, he told his teammates, "I have to respect her abilities if she made it to the sectionals." He added, "If I don't consider her a worthy opponent, then she might just beat me because I didn't take her seriously enough."

He really was the best wrestler in his weight class. He pinned her in the second period, like he had done to so many of the boys he wrestled.

Claremont was in Division III, and the team won the sectional championship with six champions and three runners up. John Lester was their one third-place winner. The four Claremont wrestlers who did not place had been eliminated from further competition. They were Jim Budd, Donnie Jones, Bob Packard, and John Thompson. Bob Packard was a freshman like John, and John Thompson was in the tenth grade. Both had shown some promise for next year's team. The six champions were Bill Thomas, Freddie Sommers, David Sommers, Lucas Kelly, Jim Hauser, and Jim Flaherty.

Billie Mayfield, Marty Zone, and Frankie Scaletti had all lost in the finals and finished second. John had some trouble against a pretty good wrestler who was a senior at 106 pounds. He lost 9-3 but wrestled well enough to come through wrestle-backs to finish third. All of the wrestlers on the team, including the ones who did not place in the tournament, continued to practice every day after school in order to help their advancing teammates.

Chapter 23

The team, going into the District Tournament with ten wrestlers, felt very confident. They all thought that if they wrestled up to their potential, they might be able to win the district championship as well.

The first round of the district tournament was set up so the champion of one of the sectional tournaments wrestles the sixth place finisher of the opposite sectional tournament. The second place finisher then wrestles the fifth place finisher from the other sectional tournament. The third place finisher wrestles the fourth place finisher from the other sectional tournament.

Coach Smith said, "This is called cross bracketing. It's done this way so hopefully the best wrestlers will meet in the district finals. It does not always work out this way, as it's possible for a really good wrestler to lose in the sectional tournament due to not feeling well, or perhaps, he just made a mistake at the wrong time and lost to someone he really could have beaten if he had wrestled up to his full potential."

Usually at each of the three levels—sectionals, districts and state—the wrestlers are paraded out to the mats, and everyone is introduced to the crowd by weight class. They start with the lowest weight at 106 pounds, and go on up to the heavyweights. The boys come out to the center of the mat when their names are called, they shake hands with their next opponent, and then they return to the side of the mat until all weight classes have been introduced.

The first round of the district tournament was an excellent one for the Claremont team. Everyone, including the boys who finished second in the sectionals, all defeated their first round opponents. Bill Thomas was outstanding as he pinned his opponent in the first period in the first round by using a head under the arm to a half nelson.

Four of the other eight wrestlers also pinned in the first round. Two of the other four wrestlers won by a major decision, beating their opponents by eight points or more. This gave their team an extra half team point. These extra half points can make a big difference in which team ends up winning the championship. John managed to get by his first round match as well, winning by a score of 7-5.

During the second round, John met a wrestler who was an eleventh grader from the opposite sectional. He lost in a well fought match by a score of 8-6. This put him in the consolation bracket and meant he would have to really wrestle well to finish in the top six places. Finishing in the top six means he would advance to the state tournament in Columbus, Ohio, at the OSU field house.

Bill continued to defeat everyone he wrestled, mostly by pinning them. He was rapidly making his way into the Championship finals. He was also continually giving support to his best friend, John. John was able to win his next two matches and wrestled his way into the finals, where he would be trying for a third or fourth place finish. This would get him to the next level, the state tournament.

"Ready, Wrestle"

John was doing very well because he had taken to the sport immediately, but the other reason he was doing so well had to do with his weight training. He had added muscle to his smallish frame, and was now actually weighing in at 105 pounds. He had increased his strength tremendously since he first began using the weight room.

Chapter 24

Claremont went into the finals with a lead that would make them hard to catch for the championship. All of the other teams were basically wrestling for second place. However, Coach Smith said to them, "Whatever you do, don't go into this round thinking you have the championship all sewed up. You all need to wrestle your best to make sure we can win the district crown." All of the boys said they would keep their heads in the matches at all times.

John went into the finals trying to get into third place. His match was a tough one, but he wrestled what may have been his best match since his sectional final match. He managed to swarm all over his opponent, taking him down, letting him go, and then taking him down again, almost at will. As the match entered the third period, he really opened up and pinned his opponent using a simple arm bar and a half nelson. He was going to the state tournament in his first year of wrestling! This is not something that normally happens to a ninth grader. Most boys who go to State have wrestled for many years before they even get to the high school level.

The other five wrestlers, who won the sectional championship in their weight class, also won a district title. Bill was almost as free wheeling in his match as John had been in his. He had pinned his way to the district championship. The only points some of his opponents received were kick out points. These are points he gave up by taking them down for two points, releasing them for one point, and then doing it again and again. He was proving he was the best wrestler in his weight class.

All ten of the boys who came to the districts were going to the state tournament the next weekend. The coaches were all extremely happy with the way the team had wrestled. They were almost afraid to say anything that might jinx them, but they all thought they had an excellent chance to win the state championship the next week. No other team had as many wrestlers going to the State tournament as they had.

Chapter 25

All of the boys were ecstatic about going to the state tournament, but they still had to go to class and do their homework. Everyone in the school was treating them like they were special.

The coaching staff did its best to make sure the team was not getting big heads for having won the district championship. Their other teammates were still coming to practice to help prepare them for the state championship.

When it was finally time to go to the tournament, the school provided buses for the team, other students, and the parents who wanted to go as well. Many families chose to drive to the tournament instead of going on the buses, but there were still five busloads of people going to the tournament from Claremont.

"Ready, Wrestle"

John and Bill's parents had become very close friends over the length of the wrestling season. They had chosen to drive to Columbus together so they could talk along the way. John's mom said to Bill's mom and dad, "I think it's wonderful how close friends our sons have become. They are almost like brothers. I hope that never changes."

Bill's mom said, "Yes, that's wonderful, and it's also terrific that their friendship has made the four of us closer too." The Lester's both agreed with her.

The ten boys going to wrestle in the tournament were pretty quiet on the way. They all had actually brought school work with them to keep them occupied, which also helped keep their minds off of what was about to happen to them. A few of them had placed in last season's tournament, and their Heavyweight, Jim Flaherty was a returning champion. They all felt they had enough wrestlers competing to be considered the favorites to win the state championship in their division.

Bill and John were sitting together on the bus and their conversation was quiet, almost as though they were in school and loud talking was not allowed. John said to Bill, "I'm really happy you suggested that I should go see Coach Smith before the season started."

Bill said, "I want to congratulate you on how quickly you picked up the sport."

They were going over the teams that had wrestlers going to the tournament. Bill had been seeded number one in the 113-pound class, having gone undefeated for the whole season. John was seeded number five in the 106-pound class. Not too bad for a ninth grader who had never wrestled before November of last year.

The finals were being held in early March. John realized that two of the boys he had lost to in the sectionals and districts were still alive in his weight class. He said to Bill, "I know I'm really going to have to wrestle well if I'm going to place."

Bill responded, "Just keep your head in the matches and you'll do fine. You've certainly come a long way since your first practice."

They finally arrived at the athletic complex in Columbus, Ohio where the state finals would be held. This was going to be a very big weekend, as all three divisions, I, II, and III, were being held in the same building. As they entered the OSU field house, everyone started shaking hands with wrestlers they knew from other schools and in some cases, other divisions.

Chapter 26

The state tournament was run slightly different then either the sectional and district tournaments had been run. The state tournament would be a three-day tournament instead of just two days. Also, the initial weigh in time was Wednesday evening instead of Thursday morning. Then wrestling would begin on Thursday. It seems as though the change would be easier for the wrestlers to make weight the night before wrestling would start. However, they would still have to weigh in and make weight on both Friday and Saturday morning.

On Thursday morning, when the wrestlers all started to arrive at the field house, many of them were in awe of the size of the area. There was enough room to have 9 mats available for wrestling at the same time.

Bill had been there before, so he knew what to expect. John, never having seen anything like this, was staring in wonder. Bill could tell he was very nervous about the size of the arena so he said to John, "Remember, the mats are all the same size as the ones we wrestle on every day at practice."

John laughed and told Bill, "That helped me to calm down a little." He realized that Bill was right in what he had said. It was still a lot to take in for someone who had only been wrestling for a few months. Regardless of his excellent record, he was still nervous. After all, there were two wrestlers in his weight class who had already beaten him along the way.

The five boys from Claremont, who had won the district championships, were all seeded number one at state. This included Bill Thomas, Freddie Sommers, David Sommers, Lucas Kelly, and Jim Flaherty.

Billie Mayfield and Frankie Scaletti were seeded third. John Lester and Marty Zone had been seeded fifth. They all needed to wrestle their best if they wanted to bring the State Championship back home to Claremont High. While they had the most wrestlers who were seeded number one, there were three or four other teams who had six or eight participants still wrestling.

Coach Smith said, "If those teams with several wrestlers do well, they can catch us if we slack off the least little bit. It's important that all of you give it your best effort the next three days."

At 8:00 a.m. on Thursday morning, the Claremont team was all dressed in their uniforms. The coaches called the boys together and did what they normally did before each match. They gathered together and had a moment of silence. They could pray, ask that all participants do their best, ask that no one get injured or just remain quiet and think about what was going to happen in a short while from now.

Coach Smith said to the team, "I really want you to pay attention to the announcer so no one misses hearing which mat you have to report to when your name is called. With all the noise, it's possible to miss your mat number if you are not paying attention."

At 8:30, all of the wrestlers in each division had to report to the main arena. At 9:00 a.m.,

"Ready, Wrestle"

the 106-pound wrestlers were announced, and were told to report to the proper mat. Three of the mats would be used for Division I, three for Division II, and three for Division III. All of Division III's matches would take place on mats number four, five, or six.

Prior to starting the matches in tournaments, each boy is designated either home (Green), or the visitor (Red). They each wear a red or green anklet. Most often, the official scorer will try to match the anklet to the color of the wrestler's uniform. This helps the referees and the scorekeepers in scoring the match. The referees wear a green wristband on their right wrist and a red wristband on their left wrist.

When points are scored, the referee will point to the wrestler who is getting the points with one hand. At the same time, he holds up the arm with the correct color of the wrestler who has scored the points, and the number of fingers held up show how many points that wrestler is to receive. With this system, there are usually very few, if any, mistakes in scoring each match.

Chapter 27

The Claremont team colors are red and white, so whenever possible, they would be given the red anklet and be considered the visiting team.

John would be the first one to wrestle and he would be on mat number five. He would be wrestling a tenth grader who had been the champion at his district meet. The boy he was to wrestle was from a Division III school that had fewer boys than Claremont had. Most of the other schools in their division, at the state meet, were about the same size as Claremont or smaller. Coach Smith thought John would have a good chance to win his match and move into the second round.

The referee made sure both boys were ready, and on their respective lines before he blew his whistle to start the match. John was very aggressive and went right after the other boy. He was able to take him to the mat using a double-leg takedown. This earned him two points. He used both hands on one of the boy's wrists and pulled the wrist toward him, using the rolling motion with his own hands and wrists. He had been taught this move the first day of practice all those months ago. At the same time, he pushed hard with his knee against the boy's buttocks.

This maneuver brought the other wrestler's arm closer to his body, and helped flatten him face down on the mat. This allowed John to remove his right hand from the wrist of his opponent and move slightly to the right side of him, while maintaining his grip with the left hand. Then he immediately put in a half nelson with the right hand and arm. He turned his opponent to his back and held him there long enough to earn John a three point near-fall. The boy finally fought off of his back before John could pin him. John rode him out for the rest of the first period. At this point, he was leading by a score of 5-0.